Sarah Maringele

AF786364

European Human Rights Law

The work of the European Court of Human Rights illustrated by an assortment of selected cases

Anchor Academic Publishing

Maringele, Sarah: European Human Rights Law. The work of the European Court of Human Rights illustrated by an assortment of selected cases. Hamburg, Anchor Academic Publishing 2014

Buch-ISBN: 978-3-95489-231-0
PDF-eBook-ISBN: 978-3-95489-731-5
Druck/Herstellung: Anchor Academic Publishing, Hamburg, 2014

Bibliografische Information der Deutschen Nationalbibliothek:
Die Deutsche Nationalbibliothek verzeichnet diese Publikation in der Deutschen Nationalbibliografie; detaillierte bibliografische Daten sind im Internet über http://dnb.d-nb.de abrufbar.

Bibliographical Information of the German National Library:
The German National Library lists this publication in the German National Bibliography. Detailed bibliographic data can be found at: http://dnb.d-nb.de

All rights reserved. This publication may not be reproduced, stored in a retrieval system or transmitted, in any form or by any means, electronic, mechanical, photocopying, recording or otherwise, without the prior permission of the publishers.

Das Werk einschließlich aller seiner Teile ist urheberrechtlich geschützt. Jede Verwertung außerhalb der Grenzen des Urheberrechtsgesetzes ist ohne Zustimmung des Verlages unzulässig und strafbar. Dies gilt insbesondere für Vervielfältigungen, Übersetzungen, Mikroverfilmungen und die Einspeicherung und Bearbeitung in elektronischen Systemen.

Die Wiedergabe von Gebrauchsnamen, Handelsnamen, Warenbezeichnungen usw. in diesem Werk berechtigt auch ohne besondere Kennzeichnung nicht zu der Annahme, dass solche Namen im Sinne der Warenzeichen- und Markenschutz-Gesetzgebung als frei zu betrachten wären und daher von jedermann benutzt werden dürften.

Die Informationen in diesem Werk wurden mit Sorgfalt erarbeitet. Dennoch können Fehler nicht vollständig ausgeschlossen werden und die Diplomica Verlag GmbH, die Autoren oder Übersetzer übernehmen keine juristische Verantwortung oder irgendeine Haftung für evtl. verbliebene fehlerhafte Angaben und deren Folgen.

Alle Rechte vorbehalten

© Anchor Academic Publishing, Imprint der Diplomica Verlag GmbH
Hermannstal 119k, 22119 Hamburg
http://www.diplomica-verlag.de, Hamburg 2014
Printed in Germany

Dedicated to my friends,
unicorns, coffee&chocolate.
I truly do love you.
Thanks.

A special thanks and my entire appreciation goes to my grandparents,
Reinelde and Andreas Maringele,
for their unconditional love.

I want to address a thanks in particular to
Stefan for the constructive remarks and coffee-parties,
Conny for being part of the duo-infernale,
Bösch for his awesomeness
and
Koni for her motivation.
Guys, you are special.

I also want to thank
Ursula Bast, Klaus Hofer, Ilse Meckler,
Manuela Ulrich, Christian Sonnweber and Doris Hangel
for being such marvelous supporters.

I am very grateful for the encouragement of
Emil, Vroni and Anna.
Thanks for all the moments of trust, laughter and happiness.

Table of contents

List of abbreviations

CEDAW	- Convention on the Elimination of all Forms of Discrimination against Women
ECHR	- European Convention on Human Rights
ECtHR	- European Court on Human Rights
EEC	- European Economic Community
EG	- Europäische Gemeinschaft
EU	- Europäische Union
ICCPR	- International Covenant on Civil and Political Rights
ICESCR	- International Covenant on Economic, Social and Cultural Rights
ICJ	- International Court of Justice
NGO	- Non Governmental Organization
OAS	- Organization of American States
PCC	- Press Complaints Committee
PCIJ	- Permanent Court of International Justice
TEU	- Treaty on European Union
TFEU	- Treaty on the Functioning of the European Union
UDHR	- Universal Declaration of Human Rights
UN	- United Nations

Preface

December 1948 is a remarkable date in the history of human rights law. It was the birth of Human Rights Law. Without exception, human rights belong to every single human being. The eighth secretary General Ban Ki-moon clearly found an adequate description to illustrate the significance of human rights while giving a speech at the 2011 Human Rights Day. Besides the significance of their existence he focused on their constant development and practicable usage which requires all the nations to exercise human rights. His speech can be put in one significant sentence. "But unless we know them, unless we demand they be respected, and unless we defend our right -- and the right of others -- to exercise them, they will be just words in a decades-old document." [1] So this led to a few questions:

Now, as we happen to have Human Rights Law in Europe what are the consequences regarding the jurisprudence and the legal practice in general? Further on, what are the judicial consequences in respect of violence against women?

How about the acquaintance within European courts especially the European Court of Human Rights Law? Did it remain the same or are remarkable changes and developments observable?

Did the development in Europe force 'us' to accommodate the understanding and meaning of what was once essential but in a completely different way?

The main focus within this work basis on the case-law of the ECtHR in order to reveal the process, development, changes and reasonings of the Court, specifically in respect of the application of the principles of interpretation. The case analyze will cover general state of affairs, e.g.: environmental issues, gender based circumstances, press related matters, physical and psychological violence in general, etc. Moreover, regarding violence, a few cases in Section Five shall illustrate the judicial approach relating to violence against women in specific; especially, since the latest violent incidents in 2013, for example in India South-America but also in Eastern Europe, revealed that violence against women is a disastrous, unsolved and widespread matter.

[1] http://www.un.org/en/events/humanrightsday/2011/sg.shtml, retrieved 20.09.2012.

Section One:

I. Introduction: the case of RTBF

As mentioned in the preface, the main purpose of this paper is to analyze how the ECtHR works, judges and which difficulties might appear. In order to understand the judgments and the legal machinery in Strasbourg, I want to start with a case; the RTBF-case. For example, one of the leading questions is, how did Human Rights Law affect the national and international jurisdiction? It becomes clear by the following example; the national courts have to consider the principles and fundamental rights, which are provided by the ECHR. On the one hand, the ECtHR investigates if the acts of the national authorities are in accordance with those principles, and, on the other hand, it examines if any interference with the fundamental rights, as we experienced in the first case, could be justifiable or not. To sum up, the ECtHR analyzes if a national judgment is legitimate or not in respect of human rights law. Of course, the ECtHR had to find its way to offer well considered judgments regarding the arguments and methods; consequently, I like to offer an insight by revealing the work in form of analyzing specific chosen cases.

We habitually consume information on a daily basis. Newspapers, television, internet, radio and other knowledge intercessional media offer all sorts of information. However, it forces the question if there are any boundaries within sharing and publishing information. To be more specific, the question is whether there should be set a boundary to restrict and control individuals, companies and groups of individuals or not. For example, in one case the European Court decided on an application from the RTBF in which the public broadcasting company of the French Community in Belgium alleged a violation of the freedom of expression[2]. As to the facts: the company broadcasts a program which is dealing with judicial matters. Part of their reveals contained concerns regarding medical risks and similar topics. Therefore they brought up an example. The company showed complaints by patients about their treatment and doctors. It should be noted that these issues have been reported before within the newspapers (printed media). The accused doctor submitted the case to the Court. After this reaction the responsible judge granted an interim injunction, preventing the company from broadcasting this program, until a decision has been made on the merits. Decisions have not been made by the time the case had been lodged with the European Court. The focus was laid on the interim injunction. First, RTBF alleged to be violated in their right of access to a Court by exhibiting Article 6 of the Convention. The Court of Cassation did not consider the fact that the claimant did bring up the possible violation of Article 10 of the Convention. The legal basis needed

[2] e.g.: http://echr.coe.int/NR/rdonlyres/C3804E16-817B-46D5-A51F-0AC1A8E0FB8D/0/DG2ENHRHAND022004.pdf, retrieved 17.12.2012.

to be questioned, because the constitution of Belgium authorizes the punishment of offending medial behavior in practicing the freedom of expression. But the main point is that it is only punished after it has been committed. Hence, the Court tried to figure out whether there is a clear, specific and certain legal base within the Civil Code or not. Such an intervention cannot suffer from a leaking judicial base, because it would mean that the conviction is an act of preventive judicial activism which obviously would not stand any further investigation. The Court found that the company was unable to foresee the consequences, because it simply was not clear enough. [3] For example there has not been any case- law by that time, so how should RTBF possibly know the precise regulation of the law? This leads to the conclusion that it simply is preventive. This conviction probably would keep many people in a safe position, just because they are aware of criticism in the media. Well, we could say that the content deals with an announcement to clarify the judicial handling in advance. But can this be the judicial acquaintance with such matters? During the further procedure the Belgian judge declared that there is a difference between print media and non print media. This unreasonable distinction has been implied by not investigating print media provider, which revealed such problematic matters several times before but judging non print media in the same field of disclosures. The Court analyzed the handling and found that there is no such legal framework, which offers the requiring base to distinguish between the two media sectors. In conclusion the Court found the Belgian State guilty for prohibiting in such a way without legal base or specific terms in the case-law by violating Article 10 of the Convention. They did not find any judicial prove for allowing such a kind of censorship. And to mention again, it seemed to involve a prior prohibition. The Constitution, combined with the Civil Code, does not offer the required fundamentals to legitimate the judgement. Therefore it is not possible for any individual to evaluate whether the content of their work is 'legally covered' or not. Hence, the Court revealed a violation of Article 6 ECHR as well.[4]

[3] RTBF v. Belgium , judgment of 29.3.2011, ECHR.
[4] RTBF v. Belgium , judgment of 29.3.2011, ECHR.

Section Two:

I. The significance of Universal Human Rights Law

Before I start with the analyzes of the case-law of the ECtHR, it is unavoidable to have an overview regarding Human Rights Law in general, important organizations and institutions as well as significant mechanisms within the international and european sphere. Therefore, I will begin with an introduction to the functioning and impact of International Organizations, the United Nations and the European Union.

There is not a particular event or a single date to enumerate. It took its time to establish Human Rights. Therefore to mention one of the more important and obvious events which influenced the European movement drastically. For example, the United Nations General Assembly, now including 193 members, held its first session in 1946.[5] In 1948 the Universal Declaration of Human Rights (Res 217 A III) entered into force.[6] The competence is widespread in consideration of 'ratione materiae'. Its practical purpose is to define recommendations and initiate field studies in reference to Human Rights questions. More specifically spoken, the Charter contains political, social, civil as well as economic and cultural rights. The legislative structure, work and progress stretches itself throughout the decades. The main matter is allegorized through legally non-binding statements, manifested in Article 10 and 13 of the Charter of the United Nations where it says '...and assisting in the realization of human rights and fundamental freedoms...'. [7]

Resolutions are not enforceable by law, which logically leads to the questionable fact that some rights are well accepted and some vary depending on the concrete legal system of the Member State. The limitation caused by national politics and legal structure is quite delicate. Regarding the implementation of international Covenants it is precarious. De jure the essential function needs to be seen in the advisory and monitoring role of the UN. For example, during Gulf war II and III, the Security Council of the United Nations 'legislated' Resolution 660. This resolution basically condemned the invasions of the Iraq and announced immediate withdrawal, combined with undertaking international negotiation. [8] To put it into one phrase, the Council tried to build international peace and security. It could be spoken of an international mediator who claims communication, emphasis on peace keeping work and the practice of Human Rights law.

---

[5] e.g.: Peterson M. J., *The United Nations General Assembly* (2006).
[6] e.g.: Johnson M. G./Symonides J., *The Universal Declaration of Human Rights: A history of its creations and implementation 1948 - 1998* (1998).
[7] The United Nations Department of Public Information, *The United Nations and Human Rights 1945 - 1995 Volume VII* (1995), *p. 143.*
[8] S/Res/660 (1990).

II. Human Rights Law on appropriate scales

A. International perspective of Fundamental Rights

1. An international mechanism

Human Rights do concern all of mankind, therefore, they are best protected on an international scale. As the main focus of this work lays on the ECHR, the detailed abstract concept of the international Law is shortened. A significant number of International Organizations grew within the last decades, not only IGO's, but also the amount of NGO's fluctuated surprisingly after

World War II, the later break down of the Soviet Union and the end of the Cold War. The influence was enormously triggered by uncertainty, the experience of War, deprivation, depression, misery.

On the ground that both, International Organizations and States, are mentioned in this study, I want to offer a short insight regarding the legal status and differences of the two of them, hence a better understanding of their legal acts is guaranteed.

a. International Organizations and International Law

International Law constitutes International Organizations as independent actors whilst States could be named as their founding-fathers at the same moment as being their members. Independence has to be understood in the sense of being constituted as a corporate person comparable with national commercial law. This leads to the fact that IGO's can allege violations, but also can be accused of violating any law, furthermore, they have a legal basis, which means that IGO's do have to comply with the rights, are addressees of obligations, but also of specific rights. To put this into one sentence 'Inter-State organizations are legally independent to their founders. Some of this independence is written into the treaties that establish them, and some of it arises by implication.'[9] Regarding independence, the Courts are constituted on this thought, meaning their power to judge as well as the argumentation leading to the judgments has to be seen separate from the Member States and from the individuals. The founders of International Organizations simultaneously can act as their members. This fact is of great significance regarding profound political and economic interests. Additionally, a State can easily refuse a Membership of an IGO, due to its sovereignty. If a State does refuse the Membership, the international Law, which is set by the IGO, is not binding. Firstly States can refuse a Membership en bloc, secondly States can consent to be a member of an IGO with reservations. The latter leads to the effect that specific conditions stipulated are legally non-binding. International Law rests on a consensus, so it could be said that it is coordinating the

[9] http://www.journal-iostudies.org/sites/journal-iostudies.org/files/JIOSfinal_3_1.pdf, retrieved 31.08.2013.

international relations and guarantees a harmonic functioning. None the less, because of the absence of a supreme authority within international law, the distinction between national law and international law has its impact; consequently specific parts and legal acts of the international law are quite often classified as soft law, which is highly controversial by the reason that a sharp distinction has to be made on the ground that not the entire acts are soft law in this sense.[10]

aa. Excursus: Conditions according to the principles of Law: IGOs and States

The United Nations, for example, is a generally accepted International Organization with the legitimation of acting in legal matters. If both, States and International Organizations, are in charge of establishing legal basis - are they the same? The Charter of the UN manifests their ability to set recommendations but a recommendation certainly is not the same as a national binding law. So, it is not a legislation in terms of our national thoughts of legislation. The UN is allowed to provide protection and intervention in cases they have the given power from the specific State which means the UN is not allowed to launch a strike without permission. It is an existing enforcement power and a constricted area of acting in terms of an intervention. Again it reveals the slightly hidden difference between States and International Organizations. Moreover, States do not need to be founded. If the international accepted criteria - State territory, State authority and citizenship - are fulfilled the consequence are e.g. unquestionable powers in legal matters. In contrast to that, International Organizations need to be founded by States; logically they lack from those three mentioned criteria above. The most effective impact is the legal issue as States have unquestionable powers regarding their territory and their citizens. International Organizations, on the contrary, have the power the members and founders assign them. That means the power is a derivative transferred power. But another distinction has to be made regarding supranational and the intergovernmental acting. Due to the fact that treaties are the most common instrument in order to achieve the targeted anticipations it is necessary to distinguish the impact of a treaty. The European Union, as an outcome of the former European Community, is endowed with supranational power, in fact, they are constituted by international treaties but they are still an agreement between sovereign States. The primary law manifests a kind of constitution due to the provision of a certain level of law and democratic tools and therefore it is far more reaching and affecting. A legal act yields immediate effect to its addresses. If specific legal acts are neglected or ignored by the members this simply leads to sanctions e.g. penalties, law-suits, indemnity claims. On the other hand, the intergovernmental treaties, e.g. the treaties of the UN, do not state any kind of constitutional basis but set binding rules for the peaceful functioning of the humankind in sense of a political, social, govern-

[10] e.g.: Slomanson W.R., *Fundamental Perspectives on International Law* (2011).

mental, legal and economical matter. In contrary to the European Union, the UN is not allowed to question the power of the contracting States and as a result of the sovereignty it can release recommendations but no legally binding sanctions. This reveals that treaties have different impact although, both are released by International Organizations. To put this into one phrase: States are the founding-fathers of institutions and institutions among each other distinguish themselves through the different kind of power given by States.[11]

2. The United Nations

The United Nations as the follower of the League of Nations, currently has 193 Members and 2 permanent observing States. [12][13] Established in 1945, when 50 countries met at the UN conference to draw up the Charter of the UN. As mentioned before, after 1945 it became clear that human rights needed to find a fixed and solid base. Human rights can resist cases of extremities only if they are implemented in legally binding structures.

Boutros Boutros Ghali, former United Nations Secretary-General, put it that way when giving a speech at the World Conference on Human Rights in Vienna in 1993 'When sovereignty becomes the ultimate argument put forward by authoritarian regimes to support their undermining of the rights and freedoms of men, women and children, such sovereignty- and I state this as a sober truth - is already condemned by history.'[14]

a. The Charter of the United Nations

The Charter regulates the relations between the Member States in certain fields; handling issues with specific chosen instruments. At the time of founding the Charter after World War II, the main goal was to guarantee equality, safety and security to act preventive against any riots which could possibly lead to a war like situation. As the preamble of the Charter already manifested 'We the peoples of the United Nations determined to save succeeding generations from the scourge of war, which twice in our lifetime has brought untold sorrow to mankind, and to reaffirm faith in fundamental rights, in the dignity and worth of the human being, in the equal rights of men and women

---

[11] Jordan R.S., *International Organizations: A Comparative Approach to the Management of Cooperation* (2001).
[12] http://www.un.org/en/documents/charter/, retrieved 21.07.2013.
http://www.un.org/en/, retrieved 26.07.2013.
[13] Observing State: The UN guarantee those two States (Holy See and the State of Palestine) e.g. the right to participate, observe, sign on resolutions, submit amendments and drafts. But there do not exist voting rights in terms of resolutions or other similar issues.
[14] http://daccess-dds-ny.un.org/doc/UNDOC/GEN/G93/142/39/PDF/G9314239.pdf?OpenElement
http://ap.ohchr.org/documents/alldocs.aspx?doc_id=5820, retrieved 21.07.2013.

and of nations large and small, and to establish conditions under which justice and respect for the obligations arising from treaties and other sources of international law can be maintained, and to promote social progress and better standards of life in larger freedoms,...'.[15]

Adopted by the General Assembly in 1948[16], it represents the first globally developed document of fundamental rights by which the entire humankind inherently is legally covered. It has been described as a constituting device, pointing out the set obligations amongst the members and the UN agreed rights regarding legal instruments, sanctions and recommendations, jointly chosen aims in terms of e.g. social, environmental, educational, humanitarian, economical and legal matters. Furthermore, the Charter contains the principles of international interaction intent on the sovereignty of each State, therefore obviously coping with the idea of equality and the fact that the UN is not setting any violating actions, as long as they are against the intent aims.[17]

aa. The purposes and principles of the Charter

The purposes and fundamental issues of the Charter can be split into the following groups:

The Charter organizes the cooperation in problematic situations between States regarding humanitarian, economic, social and fundamental rights matters.

In addition, the Charter has the purpose to offer an adequate mediation in situations of conflicts; further on, the organs act as a harmonizer of actions between the Nations.[18]

An other purpose of the Charter is to be a developer for international relations in the sense of promoting equality.

Besides that, the UN functions as a 'Human Rights Watch' and as a peacekeeper.[19]

---

[15] in Appendix.

[16] Adopted by a vote of 8 abstentions, 0 votes against it and 48 in favor. The Soviet Union, Saudi Arabia, Ukrainian SSR, Byelorussian SSR, People's Federal Republic of Yugoslavia, People's Republic of Poland, South Africa and Czechoslovakia. Reasons for the abstentions quod vide in The United Nations Department of Public Information, The United Nations and Human Rights 1945 - 1995 Volume VII (1995).

[17] e.g.: Jayawickrama N., *The Judical Application of Human Rights Law* (2002), p.25 and p.130.

[18] A/Res/62/228 (2007).

[19] Criticism was brought up by several authors regarding the question whether or not the UN offers a sufficient peacekeeping:
Maurice B., *The UN as an Organization. A Critique of its Functioning* in M. Bertrand, D. Warner, *A New Charter for Worldwide Organization?* (1995), p.359.
'To ensure real defence of democracy, human rights and peace, the establishment of an entirely new worldwide organization is indispensable, the main features of which are easily identifiable. The need for coordination at the global level should lead to the institutionalization of regular summit meetings between representatives of the major countries and the diverse regions of the world. The development of democracy should eventually emerge with regard to representation of people at the world level.'

Fundamental principles due to the Charter, for example, do contain amongst others:
The work of the UN has to be based on the principle of equality and sovereignty of each individual Member. On the other hand, the Members are obliged to set their behavior according to the principles of the Charter. If international disputes are coming up, they have to be solved by peaceful acting and intention in fact to endanger global peace. The acquired actions should be based on global justice, security and faith and besides, the Members are requested to assist the UN to guarantee the promoted rights. As a result of sovereignty and the lacking supranationality of the UN, it is not permitted to undermine a States position. Furthermore, the Charter itself does not establish any kind of authorization whereupon the UN is allowed to set a intervention as long as it concerns the national jurisdiction of a State.[20]

The Charter is separated into 19 Chapters. Chapter I and II regulate the Membership and the Purposes and Principles of the UN. Chapter III to IV concentrate on the Organs of the UN. Chapter V describes the requirements of the Security Council. Chapter VI to XIII manifests specific obligations like the determination of disputes, actions with respect to threats to the peace, breaches of the peace and acts of aggression. Furthermore, the Security Council shall define and set up the required settlements. But also act regarding regional arrangements. As stability and well-being are essential goods to guarantee peace International economic and social co-operation shall be stimulated. Economic, health, cultural, environmental, educational problems shall be investigated and solutions shall be implemented. Higher standards of living, full employment, social progress and the conditions shall be promoted as Chapter IX and X proclaim. Chapter XI to XIII reveal the trusteeship system and the Council which is in charge. In Chapter XIV the International Court of Justice finds its legal basis. Chapter XV reveals the duties of the Secretariat. Chapter XVI focus on the ratification and signature, transnational security arrangements, amendments and provisions.

b. Registered and commissioned institutions of the United Nations

According to Article 7 of the Charter, the UN is obligatorily composed of six organs. The General Assembly, the Security Council, the Economic and Social Council, the Trusteeship Council, the International Court of Justice and the Secretariat. If it is to be found necessary, subsidiary organs can be established, as long as it does not undermine the rules and principles of the present Charter.[21]

[20] e.g.: Basic facts about the United Nations (2004), p.11.
[21] e.g.: Jayawickrama N., *The Judical Application of Human Rights Law* (2002).

c. The Universal Declaration of Human Rights Law

aa. General perspectives

The first draft fragmented the Charter of the UN into three parts: The Declaration, A Covenant on human rights and measures regarding the implementation. Adopted in 1948, it entered into force as a Declaration which leads to the effect that it is not binding but through the decades it appeared to approach almost the same effect as legally binding instruments because it impacted constitutions and the development of civil society regarding the knowledge about human rights and their importance. Several national constitutions reference to the UDHR or they omit a reference and contain parts of the UDHR directly in their constitutions. Although it is not legally binding, it defines and describes issues which are manifested in the UN Charter and therefore binding for the members. It sought to guarantee the general provisions of the UN and, furthermore, achieve the needed courtesy to become common standard. As result the UDHR is mediate legally binding. John P. Humphrey classifies the UDHR as an instrument to achieve an authentic interpretation of the United Nations Charter. Mostly based on the Namibia Case where the ICJ clarified '...restrictions, and limitations exclusively based on grounds of race, color, descent, or national or ethnic origin which constitute a denial of fundamental human right is a flagrant violation of the purposes and the principles of the Charter.' [22]

Other methods of interpretation are thinkable e.g. the UDHR provides the utilized instruments in order to undertake an UN conform interpretation if it comes to issues which were left undefined within the Charter, furthermore, the UDHR. The UDHR did not only affect national constitutions and the work of the UN but also the ICJ referenced the UDHR within its judicial decisions. [23] As mentioned before, the Namibia-case, the South West Africa-cases [24], where the responsible judge clarified that although the UDHR is legally non-binding it constitutes defaults of the interpre-

---

[22] S/Res/276 (1970).

[23] e.g.: Jayawickrama N., *The Judical Application of Human Rights Law* (2002), p.26.
Further reading for the first draftings in *Yearbook on Human Rights for 1947,*
(New York: United Nations, 1949).

[24] South-West Africa Cases, judgment of 18.07.1966, ICJ.
Namibia, the former South-West-Africa, has been declared a League of Nations Mandate territory after being captured by Germany. The essential principles of the Mandates System consisted in the recognition of specific rights for the inhabitants of underdeveloped territories. An advanced Nation was declared as the 'Mandatory'. The Union of South Africa has been in charge of the administrative responsibilities. After World War II, the Mandate was considered to become a United Nations Trust Territory, in order to be under UN control, which has been refused by the Union of South Africa. Furthermore, it refused the transition to independence of the territories. The ICJ ruled that there was no obligation for converting South-West Africa into a UN trust territory, but that the bondage based on the League of Nations Mandate was to be considered. The Court found that, the Mandate in question had become extinct because of the dissolution of the League of Nations but the obligation to perform compulsory jurisdiction of the Court was transferred and therefore still intact. Logically, they had been subject to the obligations and entitled provisions, under the Charter of the UN. The Respondent bound itself when ratifying the Charter while both, the League of Nations and the Permanent Court were still in existence.

tation and therefore leads to be customary law, within the Nottebohm-case it has been referred to Article 15 (1) where it says that everybody has the right of nationality and because of the immediate referring it could be seen as a basic principle.[25] The Teheran Hostages-case dealt with a human rights violation because of wrongful behavior in terms of depriving human beings from freedoms and subjugate them to physical and psychological restraint. This treatment of the government was seen as an immediate violation of the principles of the Charter as well as of the UDHR and its basic principles and fundamental rights and freedoms. [26]

The Filartiga v. Pena-Irala Case decided that torture is now officially prohibited by the law of Nations. The Court did not only refer to the Charter but also noted that the prohibition of such inhuman and cruel acts is guaranteed through other particular treaties and States verify the prohibition by their national constitutions. [27]

---

[25] Nottebohm Case, judgment of 06.04.1955, ICJ.
This case had been brought to the Court by Liechtenstein against the Republic of Guatemala. Liechtenstein claimed that the Government of Guatemala acted against the international rules of law. Guatemala alleged several reasons against the accusations, the most significant reason was that the claim was inadmissible on the ground related to Nottebohms' nationality. At the time of the dispute, he was a German national, when he applied for naturalization in Liechtenstein while having his fixed abode in Guatemala. Based on the Liechtenstein Law of 4th Janary 1934 several necessary conditions were laid down in order to achieve the Liechtenstein nationality. The Court dealt with the question, whether or not, the naturalization had to be internationally recognized. Each State decides within its domestic jurisdiction, which is settled by its legislation, the rules relating to nationality. The Court held that specific facts, which are divergent from case to case have to be considered as well, although States are in charge of setting binding rules relating to nationality. Therefore, the claim was seen inadmissible by the ICJ, on the grounds of a lacking bondage between Nottebohm and Liechtenstein. Further on, the ICJ stated that this was not inconsistent with the international law because no State can claim that the regulations which were formulated by themselves were entitled to be recognized by an other State, unless the concerned State acted in conformity with the general rules and aims.
[26] Case concerning United States diplomatic and consular staff in Tehran, judgment of 24.05.1980, ICJ.
This case had been brought in by the United States of America against Iran because of a seizure of diplomatic offices and staff Members by militant revolutionaries of Iran. The Court stated that Iran violated their obligations to the United States, thus neglected the obliged responsibilities which led to an unlawful detention. Consequently, Iran immediately was requested to release American nationals, who were held as hostages and entrust them to the protecting power due to the Vienna Convention on Diplomatic Relations. Furthermore, the Court clearly forbid the Iranian Government to subject consular and/or diplomatic staff of the United States regarding judicial proceedings. Additionally, the Court explicitly prohibited them being forced to participate in any form, e.g. as witnesses. The ICJ pronounced that Iran had to make reparation for the caused injuries.
[27] Filartiga v. Pena-Irala, judgment of 06.06.1980, ICJ.
The plaintiffs son was tortured and murdered by Pena-Irala, who was Inspector General of Police by that time. All of them were citizens of Paraguay. Filartiga brought the case to the Trial Court which dismissed the claim. The accused party moved to the United States with a visitor visa. In the US, the sister of the murdered person caused the deportation and conviction for the wrongful death of Filartiga. The Court of Appeal had to decide whether or not the law of nations had to be applied. In specific, the Alien Tort Statute says, that the district courts shall have original jurisdiction of any civil action by an alien for a tort only, committed in violation of the law of nations or a treaty of the United States. The Court declared, that the conduct alleged violated the law of nations. This was to say that, any act, which is committed by state officials against an other individual held in detention clearly violates internationally recognized human rights law, therefore the law of nations. The Court had to interpret the law nowadays as it had evolved within civilized nations, hence the United Nations Charter made it obvious that the treatment and behavior towards its own citizens had to be a matter of international concern.

bb. The Fundamental Freedoms and Human Rights of the Declaration

The Declaration contents e.g. the following fundamental freedoms and human rights:

Article 3 contains the right to life, liberty and security of persons. The freedom of slavery or servitude is guaranteed within Article 4. Article 5 prohibits torture, cruel or degrading treatment or punishment. The right to equality before the law and equal protection before the law is ensured through Article 6 of the Declaration, further, Article 10 requires a fair trial and hearing if it comes to accusations in form of any criminal charges against an individual. Article 12 forbids any arbitrary interferences regarding a person's privacy, home or family as well as correspondence. The right to seek and to enjoy asylum is guaranteed within Article 14. Trough Article 18 the right to freedom of thought, conscience and religion is ensured. Furthermore, the Declaration requires the right to a social and international order in which the rights and freedoms recognized in the declaration can be fully realized. Article 29 orders that 'the exercise of his rights and freedoms, everyone shall be subject only to such limitations as are determined by law solely for the purpose of securing due recognition and respect for the rights and freedoms of others and of meeting the just requirements of morality, public order and the general welfare in a democratic society.'[28]

B. The European perspective of Human Rights Law

1. The European Union

a. Motives regarding the founding of the European Communities

Europe was ruled by anger, fear, poverty and, therefore, suspiciousness. As the Nazi-regime demonstrated legal structure can be undermined. Facilitation of democratic stability in Europe should be reached by establishing a wide-spread legal mandatory work. [29] 'The first alternative was to try to create Europe by means of a more or less intricate and complicated system of agreements and conventions. These could be given some cohesion by a kind of overall pact, defining general aims and attempting to harmonize them in detail. The second alternative was to create an organized Europe with a structure similar to that of a state with mandatory powers, leading eventually to a confederation or, better, a federation of Europe.' [30] Economic, social and political cooperation was crucial in order to establish a specific commonality amongst the states, hence the permanent competition which was a major factor in many outbreaks of wars. The European Communities, as

[28] Universal Declaration of Human Rights
[29] e.g.: Kesselman et al., *European Politics in Transition (2005).*
[30] Lipgens W., Loth W., *Documents on the History of European Integration, volume 3 'The struggle for European Union by political Parties and Pressure Groups in Western Countries 1945 - 1950, p. 103.*

well as the UN and the Council of Europe, were established based on the thought of cooperation and integration.[31]

aa. Excursus: The terms 'European Communities' and 'European Union'

It needs to be mentioned that these two terms strictly have to be distinguished in order to avoid misunderstandings. The establishment of the Maastricht Treaty, also known as the Treaty on the European Union brought in the term 'European Union'.[32] The Maastricht Treaty describes the fields of cooperation, the extension by the Members, additional policies, etc. Only when the Treaty of Lisbon entered into force in 2009, it became definite that the European Union is known exactly as Union. This fact was not always evident, based on the ground that the origin of the Union was considered as different. The Treaty on the European Union established three original communities; the European Coal and Steel Community, the European Economic Community and the European Atomic Energy Community. These three were brought together under the 'pillar', and consequently, the Treaty was renamed as the European Community Treaty. By the Treaty of Lisbon the 'pillar-structure' was broken up and it replaced the term 'Community' by the term 'Union', which now only refers to the European Union.[33]

b. The legal impact of the European Community on Fundamental Rights

The urgent need of the protection of fundamental rights became distinct and visible when the development of the European Community brought up new effects regarding the dimensions of their operating system. The European Community not only manifests international law, but also constitutional law for the contracting States. The consequence of the legal power of the European Community has to be considered as an enormous impact for the individuals of the Member States. Confirmed by the ECJ, this led to a new legal order, regulating the Member States as well as individuals.[34] The problematic of the newly established legal order, the impact on the European Courts as well as the judicial solutions regarding these matters can be best demonstrated by the following cases.

---

[31] e.g.: Foster Nigel, *EU Law - Directions* (2010).
[32] The Maastricht Treaty entered into force in 1993.
[33] Foster Nigel, *EU Law - Directions* (2010), p.5.
[34] e.g. Foster Nigel, *EU Law - Directions* (2010).

aa. The case of the 'Internationale Handelsgesellschaft von Einfuhr-Vorratsstelle Getreide und Futtermittel'

Before the Solange I Beschluss of Germany, the ECJ addressed fundamental rights as a general principle of law, which led to a protection through the European jurisdiction, when the ECJ had to render the judgment of Internationale Handelsgesellschaft von Einfuhr-Vorratsstelle Getreide und Futtermittel.[35] Therefore, it is important to illustrate the main arguments of the Court and the effect of the decision.

As to the facts, regarding subparagraph three of Article 12 (1) of the Regulation No 120/67/EEC of the Council on harmonizing the market in cereals the withdrawal of a license was conditional on bailing a deposit. The license was determined on the lodging of a certain deposit. The said Regulation No 120/67[36], the system of deposits should guarantee a comprehensive understanding in terms of controlling of the market trends. Furthermore, Article 9 of the Regulation No 473/67[37] only grants a forfeiture of the deposit - regarding a ceased full utilization of the license - in case of 'force majeure'. The claimant questioned the validity of the regulation of deposits. Due to these facts two questions in specific arose to the Court, first is it legal - regarding fundamental rights - to exclude a forfeiture in general although Germany implemented the Regulation and second - the exclusion - if it is not entirely effected during a valid export license? Certainly only in case of no provable fault of the person concerned.[38]

The Handelsgesellschaft did not exhaust the entire amount during the time of being in custody of the valid license neither because of any 'force majeure' nor any appreciably self-caused circumstances. The claimant alleged a violation of his fundamental national rights because of the exclusion of the forfeiture in first place. Second, the deposit more specific its amount is excessive compared to the trade margins. It could be said that the entire system of the deposit is questioned. But is a fundamental right legally binding for the judgments if it concerns the European sphere? Summarized it had to be clarified if fundamental rights, in specific the proportionality, are basis of the judgments and if so, how did the Court argue. These questions emanated from the investigation of the two policies questioned by the Verwaltungsgericht Frankfurt am Main. The system of the deposits is not to be doubted because, otherwise, the commercial intercourse would suffer from a precise control; this is indispensable for an intact import and export. The Member States and the Community need to have entire knowledge to guarantee the function of the intercourse. To cite the Courts argumentation. '[...]is essential to enable the competent authorities to make judicious use of

[35] Case 11-70, judgment of 17.12.1970, ECR.
[36] Regulation No. 120/67 of the Council of 13 June 1967, EEC.
[37] Regulation No. 473/67 of the Commission of 21 August 1967, EEC.
[38] Case 11-70, judgment of 17.12.1970, ECR.

the instruments of intervention, both ordinary and exceptional, which are at their disposal for guaranteeing the functioning of the system of prices instituted by the regulation, such as purchasing, storing and distributing, fixing denaturing premiums and export refunds, applying protective measures and choosing measures intended to avoid deflections of trade.'[39] The fact that the system of deposit could be excessive has definitely to be questioned because the burden the traders have to face simply are an unavoidable consequence of such a regulation compared to the protected general interests. Regarding the argumentation of 'force majeure' cases, the Court declared it not disproportionate since the communality of traders receive adequate protection through this provision. More likely, it has to reflect that 'force majeure' cases are limited to unusual circumstances sourced outside any possibility of controlling. Like the Court announced, 'Beyond such occurrences, for which they cannot be held responsible, importers and exporters are obliged to comply with the provisions of the agricultural regulations and may not substitute for them considerations based upon their own interests.'[40] Obviously, the Court interpreted the regulation in a certain way, which led to the fact that exceptions are strictly forbidden; otherwise the sense of the regulation would cease to exist, because the communality and not the individual interest should find protection. Another passage, where this stringent argumentation could be found, is the following; 'It therefore appears that by limiting the cancellation of the undertaking to export and the release of the deposit to cases of force majeure the Community legislature adopted a provision which, without imposing an undue burden on importers or exporters, is appropriate for ensuring the normal functioning of the organization of the market [...] '.[41]

Clearly, it denies the violation of any rights within their argumentation, but besides that the solid base for that issue has been established through that judgment. 'The system of deposits, as it is instituted by the provisions criticized, is contrary to the principle of proportionality which forms part of the general principles of law, recognition of which is essential in the framework of any structure based on respect for the law.'[42] Due to the implementation of the principle of proportionality as a fundamental right the described situation would reveal a violation of fundamental rights because they have to be considered while rendering judgments. The fundamental principles of national systems form a kind of legal basis, for instance the respect of individuals but at that stage of development the ECJ obviously manifested that the main point of view is a European one. This means that the Court has to assess and evaluate the specific circumstances of a case through 'European eyes' and not solely through arguing with national, constitutional or not, principles. 'Although Community regulations are not German national laws, but legal rules pertaining to the

[39] Case 11-70, judgment of 17.12.1970, ECR.
[40] Case 11-70, judgment of 17.12.1970, ECR.
[41] Case 11-70, judgment of 17.12.1970, ECR.
[42] Case 11-70, judgment of the Court of 17.12.1970, ECR.

Community, they must respect the elementary, fundamental rights guaranteed by the German Constitution and the essential structural principles of national law. In the event of contradiction with those principles, the primacy of supranational law conflicts with the principles of the basic German Law. [...] More particularly, the adverse effects of the system of deposits on the interests of trade appear disproportionate to the objective targeted by the regulation, which is to ensure for the competent authorities as precise and comprehensive a view as possible of market trends. It may be in due proportion to the disclosed points of the Verwaltungsgericht, but still reduced to the essence of the European thought, it has to decline the requested form of legal opinion. The validity of the act of the Union institutions can only be judged in accordance with Union law, even if they collide with national law.'[43]

Finally, it should be noted that the ECJ rejects the course of argumentation, but is about to reconsider its policy. [44]

bb. The 'Solange I Beschluss' of the Federal Constitutional Court of Germany

As mentioned above, the legal development within Europe, which mainly has been caused by the existence of the European Community and its competences, had a deep impact. The decisions the European Community draws, are widespread regarding their impact and fundamental issues; therefore, they need to be clarified on a European level in order to assure the coherence between the European Community and the Member States. Consequently, it is important to understand what specific difficulties arose within the changing legal situation.[45]

For example, Germany demonstrated that specific issue in Solange I Beschluss. The Federal Constitutional Court of Germany declared its authorization to explicitly scrutinize the compatibility of European Law and German Law in case of any objections. '[...]denn die Gemeinschaft ist kein Staat, insbesondere kein Bundesstaat, sondern "eine im Prozess fortschreitender Integration stehende Gemeinschaft eigener Art", eine "zwischenstaatliche Einrichtung"....die beiden Rechtskreise unabhängig voneinander und nebeneinander in Geltung stehen und dass insbesondere Gemeinschaftsorgane einschließlich des Europäischen Gerichtshofs über die Verbindlichkeit, Auslegung und Beachtung des Gemeinschaftsrechts und die zuständigen nationalen Organe über die Verbindlichkeit, Auslegung und Beachtung des Verfassungsrechts der Bundesrepublik Deutschland zu befinden haben.'[46] Clearly the Court illustrates the boundaries between the two scales of jurisdiction. On the one hand there exists national law and on the other hand there exists European law, in

[43] e.g.: Case 11-70, judgment of the Court of 17.12.1970, ECR.
[44] Case 11-70, judgment of the Court of 17.12.1970, ECR.
[45] e.g.: Foster Nigel, *EU Law - Directions* (2010).
[46] BVerfGE 37, 271 (Solange I).

order to harmonize their jurisdiction, coexistence has to be established, regarding the legal obligations, interpretation and acceptance of each legal core requirement. 'Die Bindung der Bundesrepublik Deutschland (und aller Mitgliedstaaten) durch den Vertrag ist nach Sinn und Geist der Verträge nicht einseitig, sondern bindet auch die durch sie geschaffene Gemeinschaft, das ihre zu tun, um den hier unterstellten Konflikt zu lösen, also nach einer Regelung zu suchen, die sich mit einem zwingenden Gebot des Verfassungsrecht der Bundesrepublik Deutschland verträgt. [...] Inzidentfragen aus dem nationalen Recht der Bundesrepublik Deutschland (oder eines anderen Mitgliedstaates) entscheidet er jedenfalls nicht mit Verbindlichkeit für diesen Staat. [...] Ausführungen in der Begründung seiner Entscheidungen, dass ein bestimmter Inhalt einer Gemeinschaftsnorm inhaltlich übereinstimme oder vereinbar sei mit einer Verfassungsvorschrift des nationalen Rechts - hier: mit einer Grundrechtsgarantie des Grundgesetzes-, stellen unverbindliche obiter dicta dar.' [47] The Constitutional Federal Court of Germany manifested their power to perpetuate the core values underlying within their jurisdiction.

The European Community, more specifically, its position within international law as well as its subsequent powers were still in progress caused by a permanent new interpretation. Hence, dissenting opinions were brought up. 'Diese Frage ist für das Verhältnis des europäischen Gemeinschaftsrechts zum nationalen Recht der Bundesrepublik Deutschland durch Art. 24 Abs. 1 GG in Verbindung mit dem Zustimmungsgesetz zum EWG-Vertrag entschieden. [...] bei sachgerechter Auslegung nicht nur, dass die Übertragung von Hoheitsrechten auf zwischenstaatliche Einrichtungen überhaupt zulässig ist, sondern auch, dass die Hoheitsakte der zwischenstaatlichen Einrichtungen von der Bundesrepublik Deutschland anzuerkennen sind (BVerfGE 31, 145 [174]). Das schließt es von vornherein aus, sie nationaler Kontrolle zu unterwerfen. [...] Die von ihnen erlassenen Rechtsvorschriften können daher in ihrer Geltung und Anwendbarkeit nicht davon abhängig sein, ob sie den Maßstäben des innerstaatlichen Rechts entsprechen.'[48] The dissenting opinion, which could not withstand the following development is predicated on the thought that the question of the compatibility and interpretation of the European law clearly has to be denied. Due to the accession to the EWG-Vertrag, the contracting Member States complied themselves to the European law, therefore, also to the European jurisdiction. Through that confession, the Member States evidently abstained from individual or general revision as to general matters, but also to individual judgments. Following the dissenting opinion, there is no further space left for national controlling of European acts.[49]

[47] BVerfGE 37, 271 (Solange I).
[48] BVerfGE 37, 271 (Solange I).
[49] BVerfGE 37, 271 (Solange I).

cc. The revision of the 'Solange I Beschluss' through the 'Solange II Beschluss'

About ten years later, in 1986 the German Constitutional Court revised Solange I Beschluss through Solange II. The crucial passage was the following 'Solange die Europäischen Gemeinschaften, insbesondere die Rechtsprechung des Gerichtshofs der Gemeinschaften einen wirksamen Schutz der Grundrechte gegenüber der Hoheitsgewalt der Gemeinschaften generell gewährleisten, der dem vom Grundgesetz als unabdingbar gebotenen Grundrechtsschutz im wesentlichen gleichzuachten ist, zumal den Wesensgehalt der Grundrechte generell verbürgt, wird das Bundesverfassungsgericht seine Gerichtsbarkeit über die Anwendbarkeit von abgeleitetem Gemeinschaftsrecht, das als Rechtsgrundlage für ein Verhalten deutscher Gerichte und Behörden im Hoheitsbereich der Bundesrepublik Deutschland in Anspruch genommen wird, nicht mehr ausüben und dieses Recht mithin nicht mehr am Maßstab der Grundrechte des Grundgesetzes überprüfen.'[50]

The Constitutional Court noted that it does not examine the legislation of the ECJ regarding the compatibility with fundamental rights guaranteed through German law. It admitted that the Community itself adequately offers sufficient protection of fundamental rights even if it is contrary to the German fundamental rights in some cases.[51]

dd. Remarks referred to the 'Solange Beschlüsse'

It is apparent from these judgments what consequences the establishment of certain institutions brought along. Clearly it was and still is difficult to bring the national interests and legal machineries in accordance with the European machinery and ideology. The Constitutional Court of Germany demonstrated that it might take its time in order to get along with these challenges. Finally, it can be said that the protection of human rights law cannot be done within a short time based on the ground that the national authorities regarding the administrative field as well as the legal and judicial field need to find their way to cope with new mechanisms and norms. Moreover, the protection of human rights and fundamental freedoms is regulated within the Member States itself on the one hand, but the European protection of these rights on the other hand, has to be implemented into the national laws, which, consequently, causes irritation and problems regarding the compatibility. The national courts are willing to reconsider their decisions and opinions as the Solange Beschlüsse did reveal.

[50] BVerfGE 73, 339 (Solange II).
[51] Case 11-70, judgment of the Court of 17.12.1970, ECR.

c. The Constitutional Law of the European Union

To understand the remarkable effect of the Union, the function of the legal machinery of the European Union needs to be understood. Three main groups can be distinguished; these are the constitutional law, the procedural law and the substantive law.[52]

The constitutional law of the Union, likewise called institutional law, can be split into three parts:

the primary law as the main source are treaties; the legal instruments, founded by the primary law, build the secondary scale.

The secondary law can find its source not only through the existence of the primary treaties, but also through unilateral agreements and conventions.

Supplementary instruments are developed by other authorities, e.g. case law by the Court of Justice of the European Union, basis requirements of international law, the principles of the Union law.[53]

d. Treaties of the Community and the impact on human rights

Before the Bill of Rights, as we know it in 2013, has been established, a few further important steps have been taken. A significant impact, regarding human rights within the Community, has been reached through treaties. Therefore, the more relevant treaties shall be discussed shortly.

The Maastricht Treaty, which entered into force in 1993, clarified that fundamental rights are guaranteed, firstly, by the Convention for the Protection of Human Rights and secondly, resulting from the particular constitutions or more precise from their traditions. Fundamental rights reached the status of being accepted as a general principle of Union law in terms of Article 6 of the EU Treaty where it says 'The Union shall respect fundamental rights, as guaranteed by the European Convention for the Protection of Human Rights and Fundamental Freedoms signed in Rome on 4 November 1950 and as they result from the constitutional traditions common to the Member States, as general principles of Community law. [...] The Union shall respect the national identities of its Member States.'[54] Clearly, the EU Treaty does not establish specific or precise formulated fundamental rights itself but only refers to the acceptance of Constitutional traditions and its effects.

---

[52] The procedural law regulates the administrative law of the European Union, moreover, it mainly comprises the actions for any judicial review of the European Court of Justice. The substantive law largely consists of secondary law and contains the legal rules which have been established in order to materialize the policies of the laws agreed under any treaty.
[53] e.g.: Foster Nigel, *EU Law - Directions* (2010).
[54] in Appendix.

Primarily, the Treaty of Nice[55] proclaimed the implementation of the Charter since then it constitutes a written legal basis for the legislation of the ECJ. After the disaffirmation of a Constitutional Treaty on European scale, the Treaty of Lisbon refers to fundamental rights. Besides developing numerous drafts, amendments and protocols to the treaties already in existence, the Treaty of Lisbon for the first time ever recognized a Charter of fundamental rights as part of the primary law; and did not only codify the existing rights. The Treaty of Lisbon combines the Maastricht Treaty and the Treaty of Rome, now known as the Treaty on the Functioning of the European Union. The Charter constitutes a Bill of Rights especially adapted to the system of the European Union. This is provided in Article 6 (1) of the Treaty of Lisbon 'The Union recognizes the rights, freedoms and principles set out in the Charter of Fundamental Rights of the European Union of 7 December 2000, as adopted at Strasbourg on 12 December 2007, which shall have the same legal value as the treaties since it entered into force in 2009.'[56] [57]

Now, as the Charter is integrated into the European code as primary law the Union's organs have decided to align their acting, not only in terms of legislation with the Charter, but also the Court, as second effect, has to strike down specific parts of the legislation if they are contravening. [58]

e. The Bill of Rights

The Charter of the European Union is recognized as the first explicitly established Bill of Rights for the Union. The document is fragmented in 6 categories: dignity, freedoms, equality, solidarity, citizens' rights and justice.

- The first fragment contains the right of life, prohibition of torture,the death penalty and slavery. Also human cloning and eugenic acts. Mostly these rights find its source in the ECHR.
- Under the second title the rights of liberty, privacy, marriage, thought, individual integrity, personal data protection, work, education, asylum, assembly and property are protected.
- The third chapter combines prohibition of all forms of discrimination regarding disabilities, age, sexual orientation, religious and cultural differences, linguistic diversities, specific rights of children as well as of elderly. Very important is the stay of equality before the law.
- Social rights and rights in the working field, e.g. fair conditions, unacceptable dismissals, payment, access to health institutions, housing assistance, are guaranteed through the fourth chapter.

---

[55] Although the Treaty of Nice was signed by the Member States in 2001, it did not enter into force until 2003 on the ground of rejections by Ireland.

[56] in Appendix.

[57] e.g.: Foster Nigel, *EU Law - Directions* (2010).

[58] e.g.: Di Frederico G., *The EU Charter of Fundamental RIghts: From Declaration to BInding Instrument* (2009).

- The fifth chapter covers administrative rights such as the right to vote, freedom of movement within the Union, the right of accessing documents.
- Through the sixth title the right of achieving a fair trial, the principle of legality, the right to an effective remedy, presumption of innocence, non- retrospectively.[59]

In its preamble the Charter declares in specific to guarantee the diversity of the cultures and backgrounds of the Member States as well as the position of the individual. An important fact is that the Treaty does not transfer more responsibilities to the Union, nor does it arise in general validity. The scope of the Bill of Rights is limited to cases where the Member State applies European Law but only then. The Charter contains two appreciably different forms of instruments, the negative and the positive rights. For the individual the positive rights impact the legally protected position, because the Member State not only has to guarantee fundamental rights but also has to set an action in the given area in order to protect the individual. The negative rights apply to the abstention of the Member State in certain fields like freedom of expression. Regarding the Member States of the Union it has to be said that the UK and Poland refused to sign parts of the Treaty therefore an exception has been made so the affected parts are not legally binding for them. The Charter is related to the ECHR, furthermore, it refers to the core rights of it. The application of the Bill of Rights does not transfer more competences than already conferred. To put it into other words: 'The Constitution seeks to combine the right of the majority to shape the development of society with the right of individuals and minorities to be treated fairly and equally. [...] It corresponds in the first instance to the parliament to identify and elaborate, i.e. to reason upon, the fundamental values that unite the members of the political community because it is the body that represents more opinions and interests than any other institution.'[60] The Charter illustrates the civic bondage between the contracting States throughout a solid base of fundamental values.

C. The European Convention on Human Rights and Fundamental Freedoms

1. The first significant measures towards an appropriate implementation of Human Rights Law

The ECHR is of great significance in general, moreover, the main focus within this work concentrates on the jurisdiction of the ECtHR, therefore, I would like to start this Chapter with some historically and legally relevant facts regarding the background of the system and operating institutions in order to fully understand the 'Strasbourg machinery' as we know it nowadays.

---

[59] e.g.: Di Frederico G., *The EU Charter of Fundamental RIghts: From Declaration to BInding Instrument* (2009).

[60] Di Frederico G., *The EU Charter of Fundamental RIghts: From Declaration to BInding Instrument* (2009), p.8 to 9.

The European Convention on Human Rights and Fundamental Freedoms opened for signature in Rome in 1950 after authorizing the Consultative Assembly of the Council of Europe.[61] [62] Regarding the situation in Europe as well as the leading aim, it definitely can be recognized as a fast process. Analyzed through the perspective of intention, it clearly could be seen as a response regarding the aftermath of the Second World War. Actually, it can be reduced to a significant fact - stable legal democracy - which literally forced the development of a functioning and peace restoring system. But not only to restore and keep freedom, but also to deliver a system which is based on the consent of all States which seemed to be the most important aim at that point.[63] It was significantly influenced by the 'Convention on the Prevention and Punishment of the Crime of Genocide' [64] as well as by the 'Universal Declaration of Human Rights '. [65]

Pierre-Henri Teitgen[66] as one of the founding fathers mentioned in 1949. '[...] with the principles of natural law, of humanism and of democracy, it would contribute to the development of their solidarity [...]'.[67] This thought can be recognized in the 'travaux préparatoires' of the ECHR.[68] The documents prepared by the Secretariat-General laconically reveal their intentions '[...]of greater unity between its members and one of the methods by which that aim is to be pursued is in the maintenance and further realization of human rights and fundamental freedoms; [...] reaffirming their profound belief in those Fundamental Freedoms which are the foundation of justice and peace are best maintained on the one hand by an effective political democracy and on the other by a common understanding and observance of the Human Rights [...].'[69] Before entering into force

---

[61] e.g.: Kleinsorge Tanja E.J., *Council of Europe* (2010).

[62] not to be confused with European Council or Council of the European Union; also see in: http://hub.coe.int/web/coe-portal/european-union?dynLink=true&fromArticleId=&dlgroupId=10226&layoutId=772, retrieved 05.12.2012.

[63] The fact that the consensus amongst the Member States is of great importance can still be found within the judgments delivered by the ECtHR. For example, when the Court notes that the Member States enjoy a certain margin of appreciation in assessing whether or not and to what extent interferences are justifiable. In the following, the Court observes if the Convention rights are still protected although interferences with those rights are given. It reiterated several times that the final decision regarding the fulfillment of the Convention requirements rests with the Court. As to the consensus, the Court has regard to the changing situations amongst the Member States, consequently, if any consensus in respect of a specific issue emerges, the Court has to consider the changed circumstances and further on it has to reconsider its assessment.

[64] The General Assembly adopted the Genocide Convention by unanimous vote of the 56 participants at its 179th plenary meeting, on 9 December 1948. After obtaining the requisite twenty ratifications required by article XIII, the Convention entered into force on 12 January 1951.

[65] also see in: *Collected Edition of the 'Travaux Préparatoires' of the European Convention on Human Rights Vol. I*: Preparatory Commission of the Council of Europe, Committee of Ministers, Consultative Assembly, II May-8 September 1949.
http://library.law.yale.edu/collected-travaux-preparatoires, retrieved 13.01.2013.

[66] Teitgen was the former Minister of Justice (1945 - 1946) and Judge on the European Court of Human Rights (1976 - 1980).

[67] e.g.: Robertson A., *Council of Europe - Collected edition of the "travaux préparatoires" of the ECHR,* (The Hague: Nijhoff M.) (1975).
http://library.law.yale.edu/collected-travaux-preparatoires, retrieved 13.01.2013.

[68] e.g.: http://library.law.yale.edu/collected-travaux-preparatoires, retrieved 13.01.2013.

[69] Nijhoff M., *Council of Europe: Collected Edition of the "travaux Préparatoires" of the European Convention on Human Rights Volume VI* (1985), p. 274.

several discussions, problematic issues and unsolved matters were brought up. The legal experts recognized the urgent need to work on legal instruments and to give access to this to individuals. This thought generated an amount of questions, reservations and negotiation among the representatives. Quite a predictable chain of thoughts obviously. How can "some paper" offer protection if individuals are excluded. Excluded in a certain way because only the powers were in charge of recognizing abuses; this lead to the fact that individuals could not specifically be protected in their rights, an inevitable circumstance caused by the wider interpretation of a unity which bound the States, although not denying their sovereignty.[70] The Convention is a document which manifests non detailed fundamental rights. So therefore, (e.g.. Art 1) it fell to the States themselves to fill in the details and to offer an effective legal system which could abandon violations.[71] Compared to the version of the Convention as we know it nowadays it presented itself as simple and in a modest way because the idea of a union was regarded with reluctant enthusiasm. Still, the Convention became the first legislative achievement within such an organization.[72]

2. The 'Strasbourg-machinery'

The non-excepted peril of being flooded by individual petitions which indeed would have nothing to do with the main purpose forced some reaction and not only, but also because the Commission was politically influenced; hence, an independent level of jurisdiction had to be built up.[73] In 2010 Protocol No. 14 entered into force. An important step has been taken, the Court now has the ability to concentrate on human rights issues or violations of urgency. Nowadays the jurisdictional system is sophisticated. It can be divided into a few sections: inter-state cases, advisory opinions requested by the Committee of Ministers and individual applications against contracting states due to violation accuses.[74] The European Court of Human Rights is a supra-national Court incorporated by the European Convention on Human Rights. The decisions made by the Court are binding for the participating states, which is a highly appreciating accomplishment compared to other treaties. Firstly, the responsibility was assumed by the Commission until 1998 when the Courts function was turned into full-time responsibility to abolish the Commissions liability in this field. This development became manifested when the Protocol No. 11 entered into force especially in Art 19. Here it says ' to ensure the observance ...there shall be set up a Court of Human Rights...' [75]

---

[70] e.g.: De Salvia M.,Villinger M. E., *The birth of European Human Rights Law (1998).*
[71] e.g.: travaux préparatoires Vol. IV.
http://library.law.yale.edu/collected-travaux-preparatoires, retrieved 13.01.2013.
[72] e.g.: Macdonald R.St.J., Matscher F., Petzold H., *The European System for the Protection of Human Rights. (1993).*
[73] e.g.: De Salvia M.,Villinger M. E., *The birth of European Human Rights Law (1998).*
[74] e.g.: Smith R.K.M., Van den Anker C., *The essentials of human rights (2005).*
[75] in Appendix.

The Convention does not only offer substantive provisions, but also assurance of the observance by each contracting state.[76] This primarily means that each state implements the provisions, in addition to any violations through trials before national authorities.[77] We are dealing with an international treaty; therefore, every single State needs to ratify the document. In case of accuses before ratification the principles are not accepted; the principles are not applicable in such a situation. This does not necessarily affect the applicant State. In fact, the ECHR covers a broad variety of responsibilities of the States. If a contracting party exercises their sovereignty with effective power outside their national border, the responsibility of them persists. A similar situation is given, in case of a continuing violation. Back then when, the institution having jurisdiction, the Commission, declared these cases admissible. But there are exceptions, for example, Turkey signed the treaty with some restrictions. An application from an individual can have a far reaching effect, as the alleged violation could have happened before the ratification and so will still be admissible.

If the remedy for the concerned matter is unsatisfactory for the injured party´s view or inadequate, or in terms of an unavailability of national procedure, the ECHR itself provides a supervisory mechanism.[78]

The European Commission was abolished therefore the Court turned into a full-time institution. But the Court suffered from a lack of effectiveness caused by the enormous number of applications. 'In recent years, however, the ECtHR has become a victim of its own success. The Court now faces a docket crisis of massive proportions, the consequence of the growing number of states subject to its jurisdiction, its favorable public reputation, its expansive interpretations of individual liberties, a distrust of domestic judiciaries in some countries, and entrenched human rights problems in others. In response to this growing backlog of individual complaints, the Council of Europe has, over the last five years, considered numerous proposals to restructure the European human rights regime and redesign the European Convention on Human Rights (ECHR).'[79] Protocol no. 11 simplified the procedure regarding the basic issues, yet still the increasing amount of workload overtaxed the resources of the Court.

---

[76] State: The responsibility is extensive. The ECHR can be applicable (needs to be settled by agreement with the contracting State after a reservation) to the entire territory of a State. Including territories for whose international concerns the contracting State is responsible for.
e.g.: The United Kingdom in respect to most of it´s dependent territories
also see in: Council of Europe, *Collected Texts, (*1994).

[77] e.g.: see in Appendix - Article 13 ECHR.

[78] e.g.: Smith R.K.M., Van den Anker C., *The essentials of human rights (2005).*
Macdonald R.St.J., Matscher F., Petzold H., *The European System for the Protection of Human Rights. (1993).*

[79] Laurence R. Helfer, *Redesigning the European Court of Human Rights: Embeddedness as a Deep Structural Principle of the European Human Rights Regime,* Vol. 19 no. 1, 125-129, EJIL (2008).

As an international organization the Council of Europe cannot set legally binding law like the UN organs can. The focus of the work relies on the thought of establishing human rights. In addition to that the Council emphasis on the co-operation between the european nations regarding cultural, democratic and social matters. The Council also operates in the range of facilitation common legal basis or standards.[80]

a. Excursus: The European Commission on Human Rights

Although the core responsibilities of the Commission were transferred, it is essential to understand the concept which built a solid base for the judicial system; hence, a short description of the Commission seems necessary.

When establishing the ECHR the European Commission on Human Rights was foreseen as a control entity of the judicial functions. The primary concept behind the formation was to build a barrier in fact, it was to stern frivolous or unfavorable petitions, which was received by the Commission. Another essential function was to provide individuals the possibility of channel law-suits against States. 'If the Court is to carry out its work effectively in every case of a violation of human rights or fundamental freedoms, access to the court must be available not only to States , but also, after an opinion has been rendered by a Committee of the Council, to individuals [...]'[81] Clearly, the Commission was oscillating between following; firstly to protect the Court from massless complaints and individuals to ensure the accessibility to the Court and secondly, to decentralize the traditional state focused on international legal mechanism. In 1994, all contracting parties had agreed to private petitions. In 1999, the entire competences of the Commission had been absorbed by the newly reformed Court of Human Rights.[82]

3. The specific Convention Rights

The Convention Rights are fully listed in the Appendix, therefore this only is an excerpt:

Article 2 protects the right to life; further in Articles 3 and 4 the prohibition on torture, inhuman or degrading treatment and slavery are covered.

Article 5 contains the right no to be arbitrarily detained, further on, Article 6 guarantees a fair trial. Within Article 7 retroactivity of criminal law is mentioned.

Article 8 and 9 protect the right to family, private life, home, correspondence and the right of thought, conscience, and religion.

---

[80] Macdonald R.St.J., Matscher F., Petzold H., *The European System for the Protection of Human Rights. (1993).*

[81] Janis M., Kay R., Bradley A., *European Human Rights Law* (2008), *p. 25.*

[82] e.g.: Janis M., Kay R., Bradley A., *European Human Rights Law* (2008).

The freedom of expression and assembly as well as association are guaranteed through Articles 10 and 11.

Article 12 constitutes the right to marry and have a family.

The right to access to domestic remedies and the prohibition of discrimination are covered through Articles 13 and 14.[83]

From Section Three onwards the focus concentrates mainly on alleged violations of Article 3, Article 8 and Article 10 of the Convention. Consequently it is required to know the specific definitions and meanings which are generelly utilized by the Court when it comes to legal analyzes.

Article 3 - Prohibiton on torture, inhuman or degrading treatment

No one shall be subjected to torture or to inhuman or degrading treatment or punishment.

Article 3 ECHR has a fundamental character, which means that no derogations are permitted in time of peace and in time of war, respectively. The impact of utilizing 'the living instrument' or in other words 'the dynamic interpretation' as a method of interpretation is massive in the case-law of the ECtHR; because the interpretation, in respect of the changing circumstances, consequently leads to different definitions troughout the time. The ECtHR refers to a definition provided by the UN-Convention against Torture and Other Cruel, Inhuman or Degrading Treatment or Punishment which descirbes the terms as follows 'any act by which severe pain or suffering, whether physical or mental, is initentionally inflicted on a person for such purposes as obtaining from him or a third person information or a confession, punishing him for an act he or a third person committed or is suspected of having committed, or intending or coercing him or a third person, or for any reason based on discrimination of any kind, when such pain or suffering is inflicted by or at the instigation of or with the consent or acquiescence of a public official or other person acting in an official capacity.'[84] The ECtHR is not articled to this definition but it was and still is a meaningful description that led to few important criteria which the EctHR emphazises on; a minimum level of severity, the act has to be based on intent, and finally the act needs to be attributed to a Member State. This leads to the effect that trivial complaints do not fall within Article 3 ECHR, unless the treatment caused severe humiliation or suffering to the victim. Regarding the distinction between the two terms, it has to be said that a distinction is not necessary, and in many cases not even possible. By definition, Article 3 ECHR only can be committed by state organs; consequently, the degrading act or interference must stem from the authorities in a certain manner.[85]

---

[83] in Appendix.

[84] The Convention was adopted by the UN-General Assembly on the 10th December 1984. It entered into force on the 26th June 1984.

[85] e.g.: Jacobs F.G., White R., Ovey C., *The European Convention on Human Rights* (2010).

Article 8 - The right to respect private, family life, home and correspondence

1. Everyone has the right to respect for his private and family life, his home and his correspondence.
2. There shall be no interference by a public authority with the exercise of this right except such as in accordance with the law and is necessary in a democratic society in the interests of national security, public safety or the economic well-being of the country, for the prevention of disorder or crime, for the protection of health or morals, or for the protection of the rights and freedoms of others.

The protection of the family can easily be found at more than only one place in the Convention but Article 8 ECHR is the most significant one. It does not exist one clear definition of the term family caused by various reasons, e.g.: the changing society, different background and culture in Europe, etc. In fact the ECtHR once said that 'the mutual enjoyment by parent and child of each other's company constitutes a fundamental element of family life.'[86] On other occasions the Court noted that a family also exists although a married couple did not set up home together. In respect of children, a family between the children and the parents is given from the beginning of life onwards. Only a few exceptional circumstances lead to the presumtion that a family, which seems to be naturally linked, is not given. Family life consequently protects the de facto relationships as well. It cannot be denied that the existence of some form of hierarchy is dominant, e.g.: if a case is brought before the ECtHR. 'At the top of the hierarchy is the traditional heterosexual relationship of married couples, moving through parenting between non-married heterosexual couples down to more removed family relationships.'[87] The pronouncements of the Court lead to the conclusion that the core was and still is very much the family in a traditional sense. Of course, further aspects need to be covered when it comes to 'family-questions', e.g.: custody, care proceedings, adoption, the rights of inheritance, acts of national authorities when it comes to expulsion of non-nationals, etc. The Court increasingly explored the scope of the protection of private life wihtin its case-law. When following one possible point of view, it actually can be said that all reasonable aspects can be reduced to five main categories; 'freedom from intereference with the physical and psychological integrity, freedom from unwanted access to and collection of information, freedom from serious environmental pollution, the right to be free to develop one's identity and the right o live one's right to live life in the manner of one's choosing.'[88] Of course, if it is unavoidable or necessary the Court adapts these categories to offer manifestly well founded judgments in respect of the situation concerned. An other author simply said that the concept of private life has not yet been conclusively defined, but it has been referred to in a wide range of contexts.'The Court has held that the notion of privacy is not limited to the 'inner circle' of an individual's private life, but includes the right to establish and develop relationships with other human beings. Private life includes physical,

[86] Jacobs F.G., White R., Ovey C., *The European Convention on Human Rights* (2010), p.335.
[87] Jacobs F.G., White R., Ovey C., *The European Convention on Human Rights* (2010), p.337.
[88] Jacobs F.G., White R., Ovey C., The European Convention on Human Rights (2010), p.357.

psychological, and moral integrity - incorporating 'multiple aspects' of a person's physical and social identity.'[89] In respect of the second point of view, this definition includes, for example, mental health, personal ethnic and sexual identity, sexual orientation, the right to establish and develop relationships with other individuals, recognition of the martial status by the states, pregnancy, a person's name, etc.[90] Regarding the term home, the Court includes, inter alia, 'permanent and temporary places of residence, offices and business premises, and also places of residence that are not legally established. [...] includes the right to enjoy the home.'[91] The right to respect the individual's home should not lead to the conclusion that the ECHR established the right to be provided with a home. Article 8 ECHR also protects a wide range of communications. For example, post, telephone, fax, e-mail or personal internet usage. Although these rights are mainly protected by other elements like the right to private life.[92]

Article 10 - The freedom of expression

1. Everyone has the right to freedom of expression. This right shall include freedom to hold opinions and to receive and impart information and ideas without interference by public authority and regardless of frontiers. This article shall not prevent States from requiring the licensing of broadcasting, television or cinema enterprises.
2. The exercise of these freedoms, since it carries with it duties and responsibilities, may be subject to such formalities, conditions, restrictions or penalties as are prescribed by law and are necessary in a democratic society, in the interests of national security, territorial integrity or public safety, for the prevention of disorder or crime, for the protection of health or morals, for the protection of the reputation or rights of others, for preventing the disclosure of information received in confidence, or for maintaining the authority and impartiality of the judiciary.

The freedom of expression has to be discussed precisely when applying other Convention rights. E.g., Article 8 ECHR is closely related to Article 10 ECHR because respecting someone's privacy is automatically linked to the freedom of expression, if the exposed information interferes with the former provision. The ECtHR reiterated that Article 10 ECHR constitutes a fundamental base in a democratic society, which also means that the freedom of speech is conducive to a person's self-fulfillment. The right includes competing values within itself, self-expression or freely flowing information and on the other hand, it manifests the social necessities or responsibilities of receivers of ideas, but also the liberty of opinion, information, broadcasting and press, film and television. The significant fact about Article 10 ECHR is its wide scope of written exceptions in favor of the Member States. 'The right to freedom of speech extends to all types of expression which impart or convey opinions, ideas or information, irrespective of content or the mode of communication.[...]

[89] Leach P., *Taking a Case to the European Court of Human Rights* (2011), p.315.
[90] e.g.: Leach P., *Taking a Case to the European Court of Human Rights* (2011), p.315.
[91] Leach P., *Taking a Case to the European Court of Human Rights* (2011), p.318.
[92] e.g.: Leach P., *Taking a Case to the European Court of Human Rights* (2011).

The right to free speech applies to 'everyone', whether natural or legal persons[...].'[93] Concerning the category of the freedom of expression two categories have been deputized, the first based on the fact that discussion to discover the truth, seen in a political sense, cannot progress as long as there is no such right to express ones opinion on particular matters and secondly expression basis on the urgent need of society to communicate emotions, considerations, opinions and ideas. As mentioned in the beginning the freedom of expression is severe limited within subparagraph two where the margin of appreciation and proportionality find quite a large general approval.[94]

a. The nature of the Convention rights

Regarding the nature of the fundamental rights, it can be said that the predomination of the ECHR is lying on political and civil rights. To analyze the jurisdiction of the ECtHR in the light of the principles (see Section Three) a further distinction has to be made. Besides the material sense within the rights they can be divided into absolute, limited and qualified rights.

Absolute rights as such are Article 2 to 4 and 7 cannot be interfered. If so, the concerned contracting party cannot justify the interference irrelevant under which circumstances the argumentation would take place; further on these rights cannot be addressed by a derogation.[95]

Two rights are mainly considered as limited rights. Article 5 and 6, the former protects from arbitrary detention and the latter ensures a fair trial; the significance of these two provisions is that the term limitation should not be misunderstood as it solely means that detentions are absolutely and strictly prohibited, only if not fulfilling the required aspects.[96]

Regarding the last category, the qualified rights, the requirements under which an interference is justified do need to cope with the interests of the community, on the one hand and those of the individuals on the other. Particularly these rights are Article 8 to 11. Significant is the mechanism behind these rights, which was developed by the ECtHR, it charges the contracting Member with the responsibility to offer certain protection but also allows him to interfere. The State can justify the concerned interference and the Court on the other hand reviews the justification respectively, the margin of appreciation and the concept of proportionality in order to offer an adequate definition, as to whether or not the justification is sustainable.[97]

---

93 Lester Anthony in *The European System for the Protection of Human Rights* (1993), p.469.
e.g.: Sunday Times v. the United Kingdom, judgment of 26.04.1979, ECHR.

94 e.g.: Lester Anthony in *The European System for the Protection of Human Rights* (1993).

95 e.g.: Janis M., Kay R., Bradley A., *European Human Rights Law* (2008).

96 e.g.: Janis M., Kay R., Bradley A., *European Human Rights Law* (2008).

97 e.g.: Janis M., Kay R., Bradley A., *European Human Rights Law* (2008).

b. Interferences with fundamental rights

As in Section Three, the jurisdiction and the case-law will be analyzed in order to unveil the system of the principles of interpretation, it is necessary to give a review concerning interferences, which may or may not be permissible. By the diversity of the legal background of the contracting parties it inevitably led to a more complex mechanism in order to satisfy the requirements of the Convention. Therefore, infringements and interferences are unavoidable. Ergo, if it comes to such an occasion it has to be justified.[98]

Firstly, an interference can be justified if it is 'in accordance with the law' which means that any arbitration of authorities has to be avoided through guaranteeing a sufficient controlling mechanism. For example, 'The expression 'in accordance with the law' in paragraph 2 of Article 8 ECHR means firstly, that any interference must have some basis in the law of the country concerned. However, over and above compliance with domestic law, it also requires that domestic law itself is compatible with the rule of law. It thus implies that there must be a measure of legal protection in domestic law against arbitrary interferences by public authorities with the rights safeguarded by paragraph 1.[99]

A further requirement is the accessibility which means that the concerned individual necessarily has to be provided with access in particular. Furthermore, the term in accordance with the law also implies that law cannot suffer from clarity. The Court formulated this requirement within the Sunday Times-case, where it says that 'In the Court's opinion, the following are two of the requirements that flow from the expression 'prescribed by law'. Firstly, the law must be adequately accessible: the citizen must be able to have an indication that is adequate in the circumstances of the legal rules applicable to a given case. Secondly, a norm cannot be regarded as a 'law' unless it is formulated with sufficient precision to enable the citizen to regulate his conduct: he must be able - if need be with appropriate advice - to foresee, to a degree, which is reasonable in the circumstances, the consequences which a given action may entail. Those consequences need not be foreseeable with absolute certainty: experience shows this to be unattainable.'[100] In some of the Conventions'

---

[98] e.g.: Janis M., Kay R., Bradley A., *European Human Rights Law* (2008).

[99] Malone v. the United Kingdom, judgment of 02.08.1984, para. 66 to 68, ECHR.
The case was brought to the Court on grounds of an interception of a telephone conversation by the Post Office on behalf of the police in charge. The interception had been authorized by the Home Secretary. The United Kingdoms Government stated that the applicant was a suspect of a theft, therefore it was justifiable to intercept his telephone and postal communications. The Government, however, did not deny nor did it admit 'metering' his communications. The ECtHR stated that there were interferences with the right to respect privacy. Consequently, the Court dealt with the question whether or not the interferences with Article 8 ECHR were in accordance with the law in respect of paragraph 2 of Art. 8. In order to accept such interferences, there have to be measures of legal protection, which contravene arbitrariness. In the specific case the Court found that to that extent, the requirements were not fulfilled, logically the interception was arbitrary and the consequences not foreseeable to the claimant. Consequently, the Court omitted whether or not the interference was necessary in a democratic society. In conclusion, Article 8 was violated.

[100] Sunday Times v. the United Kingdom, judgment of 26.04.1979, para. 49, ECHR.
This case will be analyzed in detail in a further Section.

provisions, the Convention itself offers an enumeration of aims which legitimate possible interferences. The accused State is required to prove that an infringement does satisfy a legitimate aim.[101] The characteristic of the phrase 'the necessity in a democratic society' is of great significance. The Court investigates the merits in the scope of the domestic law and weighs the need in a democratic society against the infringed fundamental right.[102]

c. Jurisprudence, qualified rights and the margin of appreciation

In Section Three the main focus lies on the jurisprudence of the ECtHR in the light of the application of the principles. Therefore, solely a brief insight should be given regarding the coherence of the particular issues.

Article 8 ECHR up to Article 11 ECHR are often discussed in combination with the margin of appreciation because of their nature as qualified in the sense of accommodated rights. Regarding the involvement of limitation clauses within those rights, severe attention has to be paid when pronouncing a sentence. The drafting is similar; the first paragraph states the provision, while the second paragraph contents particular conditions under which the contracting party is entitled to breach the negative provision. Such conditions may be 'in accordance with the law' (Art. 8) or 'prescribed by law' (Arts. 9, 10, 11); meets one of the legitimate aims; and is 'necessary in a democratic society'. The term 'necessary' implies a proportionality test and the interpretation of the phrase 'necessary in a democratic society' epitomizes the tension created by the collision between the individuals and the society.'[103] Clearly, it depends on the rights involved, as to whether or not the margin of appreciation is wider or narrower. A spectacular case was a topic in 2007, when the Court had to decide whether or not a breach of Article 8 ECHR had been given; it concerned the question of the possibility to deprive a former consent in order to hinder the usage of the genetic material until the moment of implantation. 'In conclusion, therefore, since the use of IVF treatment gives rise to sensitive moral and ethical issues against a background of fast-moving medical and scientific developments, and since the questions raised by the case touch on areas where there is no clear common ground amongst the Member States, the Court considers that the margin of appreciation to be afforded to the respondent State must be a wide one'.[104] Further on, in order to protect the morals of the contracting States the Court does tend to respect a wider margin of appreciation within its judgments especially when qualified rights are in question.[105]

---

[101] e.g.: http://www.coe.int/t/dghl/cooperation/lisbonnetwork/themis/echr/paper2_en.asp, retrieved 29.08.2013.
[102] Detailed analyzes regarding this specific issue will follow in a further Section.
e.g.: Handyside v. the United Kingdom, judgment of 07.12.2976, ECHR.
[103] http://www.coe.int/t/dghl/cooperation/lisbonnetwork/themis/echr/paper2_en.asp, retrieved 30.08.2013.
e.g.: Sunday Times v. the United Kingdom, judgment of 26.04.1979, ECHR.
[104] Evans v. the United KIngdom, judgment of 10.04.2007,para 81, ECHR.
[105] Handyside v. The United Kingdom, judgment of 07.12.1976, para 48, ECHR.

d. A continuing revolution through the implementation of Protocols

Since the existence of the ECHR 14 additional protocols have been added to the original text. In 2013 No.15 and No. 16 opened for signature; and when the ratification process will be closed, these further provisions will give Member States the opportunity to request advisory opinions from the Court regarding questions concerning the interpretation and application of the defined rights. Regarding the nature of a protocol a few facts need to be acknowledged. The protocol is a supplementary act, where to find additional rights in addition to the original text, logically it does not happen to have the nature to strike out the rights and fundamental freedoms. Concerning the status of the Member States the binding nature only appears through the acts of signature and ratification, otherwise a Member State cannot be bound to additional obligations in form of protocols.[106]

D. General aspects

1. Treaties as an instrument of Law

The most cited applications are treaties in order to achieve consolidated multilateral or bilateral international objectives. Because of the importance of treaties within the European legal sphere, especially when it comes to human rights protection, it is necessary to know the fundamental facts about the functioning of treaties. Treaties offer the possibility to retain diversity and the individual national expectations, specifically in the range of the national constitutional scale. Therefore, they are an essential tool for the purpose of preserving, developing and sensitizing contemporary international relations in order to achieve common legal arrangements. The instrument treaty is not only used in terms of political, economical or similar fields but also in social and specific in human rights scopes. Although treaties are not legally binding in the way constitutional law or other sources of law are. The absence of specific sanctions does not necessarily lead to the conclusion of the absence of a legal duty. 'The absence of any sanctions of the non-performance or violation where provision does exist for reporting, does not detract from their binding nature.'[107]

a. The ECHR as an international source of law

'The Convention represents [...] a collective guarantee in the European context of a number of principles set out in the Universal Declaration of Human Rights, supported by an international judicial machinery making decisions that must be respected by Contracting States. In this regard,

---

[106] e.g.: http://www.echr.coe.int/Pages/home.aspx?p=basictexts&c=#n13739063294958599503665_pointer, retrieved 15.12.2013.
http://www.conventions.coe.int/Treaty/Commun/ChercheSig.asp NT=213&CM=8&DF=15/12/2013&CL=ENG, retrieved 15.12.2013.
http://www.conventions.coe.int/Treaty/Commun/ChercheSig.aspNT=214&CM=8&DF=15/12/2013&CL=ENG, retrieved 15.12.2013.

[107] Jayawickrama N., *The Judicial Application of Human Rights Law* (2002), p. 84.

the most important, and most original, feature of the European Convention is the system it established for the protection of the human rights is guaranteed.'[153] In the following section the specific provisions and fundamental freedoms which were guaranteed through the Convention will be discussed and the primarily legal background will be exposed by case law focusing on the implementation of the principles, especially the margin of appreciation and the evolutive interpretation.

2. The international position of the ECHR

In general it is clear that no state can escape from the responsibility that arises from the Convention because its character is superior. Although the transmission or implementation of the provisions is part of the state's legislative freedom. '[...]but it leaves the manner in which the result is achieved to the discretion of all States concerned.'[108] It can be said that the rank of the Convention differs on the fact which dogmatic point of view is chosen as criterion, but the focus actually lies on the result. The aim is to guarantee a proper achievement of fundamental provisions, therefore, the Convention itself can be ranked between statute law and constitutional law. It also can be classified as constitutional law on the same scope as national constitutional law.[109]

a. The ECHR and domestic law

Monism and Dualism have been the most utilized instruments in order to find a dogmatic solution for the problematic place of international law and domestic law. Difficulties arise when rights need to be provided but domestic law is interfering and as a possible outcome the requirements of the Convention are not fulfilled. The emphasis in this work is given to the question 'Is domestic law compatible with the Convention? How does the Court argue in case of a collision of the two of them? The Court repeatedly announced that no general or abstract answer can be provided to that matter because it always depends on the specific case. If interferences are discovered the Court has to review whether or not the concerned law is applicable in order to achieve the provided rights.
As it will be particularly examined later, in several cases the Court found violations of the Convention because of non compatible domestic law.[110] Although the Court is a supervisor it is not in its

[108] Bernhardt R. in *The European System for the Protection of Human Rights* (1993), p.25.
[109] e.g.: Bernhardt R. in *The European System for the Protection of Human Rights* (1993).
[110] e.g.: Dudgeon v. the United Kingdom, judgment of 22.10.1981, ECHR.
The applicant filed a suit based on the circumstances that certain laws in Ireland had the effect that specific homosexual acts between consenting adult males were classified as criminal offences. Sodomy, inter-crural contact, for example, between male persons were seen as sexual indecency. Therefore, the applicant was liable to criminal prosecution by reason of his homosexual actings/behaving. The Commission and the Court, respectively, found a violation of the right to respect the applicant's private life. Further on, the Commission pointed out that the interference is in accordance with the law. Consequently, it had to be figured out whether or not the interference was targeted protecting morals or rights and freedoms of other individuals. The Court clearly adhered to former argumentations when saying that such interferences were legitimate in order to protect vulnerable individuals. It recognized the purpose of the legislation and classified the latter as a safeguard for society. Regarding the fact that the legislation had to be necessary in a democratic society, the

responsibility to generally substitute the domestic courts' interpretation without profound legal doubts. Remarkable observation within the case-law seems to be that a dualistic approach is still necessary.[111]

Court noted that the measure had to be proportionate to the legitimate aim. The change of time, morals and societal behavior had its impact, so that, such interferences, although well and carefully considered, were not necessary in order to secure national morals. Consequently, the margin of appreciation was set narrower by the Court. A breach of Article 8 was given on the grounds of classifying such homosexual acts as criminal offences.

[111] e.g.: Bernhardt R. in, *The European System for the Protection of Human Rights, 1993.*

Section Three:

I. General aspects of the jurisdiction of the ECtHR in regard of diversity

The rights of the Convention require specific interpretation in order to guarantee a stringent, adequate and wide spread validity for the application of the ECHR and also in fact to establish a legal compliance. The crux is that fundamental rights are a matter of a national margin of appreciation as well as an universal matter, but yet no consensus has been found regarding the question whether the developed principles of the ECtHR are unsatisfactory and betray the universal sense of fundamental rights. In respect of the Member States it becomes unavoidable to enable the rights divergent and consequently establish a flexible but still stringent system. The ECtHR is obliged within its judgements to define, classify and circumscribe unclear or upcoming 'termini' for the purpose of a proper application by the Member States. By recognizing the diversity of the Member States the ECtHR developed certain essential principles which shall be exposed within this section in the light of the fact that the principles are an essential judicial mechanism.[112]

A. Excursus: The third party effect

In reference to European Law especially fundamental freedoms and therefore the obligations of the Member States of the European Union, third party effect means the ability for individuals to enforce violations caused by other individuals.[113] After exposing the term to what it is, it can be said that the third party effect simply deals with the question as to whether an application to the behavior of individuals is possible or not. Obviously there are two divergent scales to distinguish between: One is the national or constitutional scale; the matter whether a State itself guarantees a third party effect within its national jurisdiction or not. The second scale, a more pre-eminent scale at this point, which struggles with the question as to when it comes into need of action by the Court of Human Rights.[114] Clearly, it can be manifested that the ECHR itself does not offer such a kind of legal instrument in particular.[115] Therefore it is a phenomenon within the national legal handling. It needs to be distinguished between the two most common terms. The representatives from the first view define third party effect as followed; human rights guarantees apply in legal issues between private parties. This means that the protection mechanism is further reaching than only between individuals and public authorities. The second view argues that individuals can enforce their guaranties against each other. Caused by the ratione personae these specific violations accuses are valued as incompat-

[112] e.g.: Greer S., *The European Convention on human Rights: Achievements and Prospects* 2006).

[113] e.g.: Frenz W., *Handbuch Europarecht, Band 5: Wirkungen und Rechtsschutz (2010),* p.326.
Ganten T.O., *Die Drittwirkung der Grundfreiheiten (2000).*

[114] e.g.: Macdonald R.St.J., Matscher F., Petzold H., *The European System for the Protection of Human Rights (*1993).

[115] e.g.: Grabenwarter C./Pabel K., *Europäische Menschenrechtskonvention: Ein Studienbuch* (2012), p.141.

ible with the ECHR. On this account the Court evaluates complaints from individuals against other individuals as inadmissible. As the case may be, it is conditionally linked to the interpretation of the Court.[116]

1. The recognition of the third party effect through the case law of the ECtHR

One of the more famous cases, where the third party effect firstly has been confirmed, shall be analyzed in order to reveal the concept properly.

a. Case of Airey v. Ireland in respect of the third party effect

In 1973, the case was brought in by the Commission because of an accusation against Ireland by Mrs. Airey, an Irish citizen. It is not only remarkable in terms of the argumentation regarding the third party effect; other circumstances need to be paid attention to, for example, the fact that the claimant is a woman who suffers physical violence and demands effective protection. Furthermore, the fact that the case has been taking place from 1973 onwards and although there is no explicit demand for the specific protection of women and the proclamation of their rights, still it can be interpreted as some fundamental first steps towards these issue. These further reaching aspects simply should be considered when analyzing case law. The focus should not lay on the formal aspects in general but only on the formal requirement regarding the third party effect.[117]

The appellant alleged that her husband, besides being an alcoholic, threatened her with physical violence in frequent intervals and also made her a subject to physical violence on several occasions. The husband was convicted by the District Court of Cork City of assault and therefore fined in 1972. The convicted husband left the matrimonial home with no signs of returning. For the reason of annulment of her marriage the appellant applied to an ecclesiastical tribunal. This step has been taken because the Irish law does not recognize a divorce in the sense of a dissolution of a marriage. There is the possibility of a decree of judicial separation made by a court or a legally binding document between the two parties. The decree can only be granted if there are circumstances like adultery, cruelty, unnatural practices or matrimonial offences. In Ireland legal aid is not granted for purposes in the sense of judicial separation. In 1976 the Family Law Act entered into force. It was only since then that financial aid was provided in family matters.[118]

She alleged the State for failing in terms of security and protection of her physical and mental integrity caused by the violation she had to face from her physically as well as mentally cruel husband. Several other complaints have been made like the protest against an unlawful detention.

---

[116] Van Dijk P./Van Hoof G.J.H., *Theory and Practice of the European Convention on Human Rights,* 3rd ed., *(1998), p.23.*

[117] Case of Airey v. Ireland, judgment of 09.10.1979, ECHR.

[118] Case of Airey v. Ireland, judgment of 09.10.1979, ECHR.

She accused the State of alleging Article 6 ECHR of the Convention, by reason of the fact that her right of access to a court was effectively denied, further, that her right to respect the privacy was violated on the ground of the denied access. More specific, the State would had the responsibility to ensure an accessible legal procedure to define such obligations and family matters. Further on, Article 13 ECHR and 14 ECHR were violated by reason of being deprived of an effective remedy within the national legal system and the lacking financial possibilities/ressources.[119]

To analyze the argumentation of the Court it needs to be laid focus on the two following Articles; Article 6 ECHR and Article 8 ECHR. Under the protection of Article 6 (1) ECHR the Court clarified, it is not sufficient that the claimant would have had to represent herself without legal support. In almost every matter of separation the petitioners had its representatives; not only this but because of the emotional involvement but also because of the lack of objectiveness of the claimant which would not be the case if the person would be represented by an advocacy before the Court. Therefore, the Court considered it unsatisfactory regarding the assumptions manifested by Article 6 (1) ECHR because the access to a fair trial is not guaranteed by the Irish system if there is no financial support. The fact that the claimant could not afford an advocate is a question of personal circumstances this is out of question but does this automatically lead to the fact that Ireland did not commit a questionable omission? It is one of the powers a State is in charge of, not to remain in silence and be a passive part. Like the responsible judge clarified 'The obligation to secure an effective right of access to the courts falls into this category of duty.'[120] An analogue argumentation regarding article 6 (3) ECHR would be impossible because para. 3 explicitly demonstrates the rights only if it comes to a criminal matter but not a civil procedure. The Court also arguments, that they do interpret the Convention so that it is not the obligation of any State to guarantee a free legal aid system. Article 6 (1) ECHR only implies that individuals need to have the possibility to access the Court. This access has to be effective but does not set any specific obligations in terms of the varieties of it. Caused by the multiplicity of types of litigations and the particulate complexity of jurisdictional procedures it could lead to the obligation that a State is forced to provide legal aid otherwise the effective access is affected. In the present case the circumstances led to the result of a missing effective access.[121]

Under the aspect of private sphere, the States may be obliged not only to guarantee to omit any kind of interference caused by themselves but also to ensure a functional system for individuals among themselves. This would be a third party effect because it imposes the States to abstain from any kind of interrupting circumstances or behavior of the privacy from other individuals. As analyzed before, the claimant did not happen to receive the access she should have. The crux is that the

[119] Case of Airey v. Ireland, judgment of 09.10.1979, ECHR.
[120] Case of Airey v. Ireland, judgment of 09.10.1979, ECHR.
[121] Case of Airey v. Ireland, judgment of 09.10.1979, ECHR.

violation which led to a breach of the right to respect for private and family life has not been set by the State or its operating institutions. So how can Ireland be responsible for that breach? Due to the unsatisfactory possibility of access she has not been able to claim for the right guaranteed by Art. 8 ECHR. Ireland is responsible to offer support to individuals so that the rights of the ECHR are effective. This is an outcome of a positive obligation, in fact to protect individuals who are victims of domestic violence or abuse. The problem is not that the State did interfere with the private sphere of the claimant but rather it did not act. Positive responsibilities are inherent to the right of private life and family, otherwise it would direct its main content ad absurdum. As three out of four Judges correctly argued 'it was not effectively accessible to the applicant : not having been put in a position in which she could apply to the High Court [...], she was unable to seek recognition in law of her de facto separation from her husband. She has therefore been the victim of a violation of Article 8 ECHR.'[122]

II. The Courts' case-law in respect of significant principles and methods of interpretation

A. The principle of Subsidiarity

'The principle of Subsidiarity is generally understood to mean that in a community of societal 'pluralism' the larger social unit should assume responsibility for functions of the unit only insofar as the smaller social unit is unable to do so.'[123] As analyzed before, it has been an outstanding revolutionary initiation to launch the European Court of Human Rights. This leads to the question if there is a potential collision of jurisdiction?

1. The implementation and effects of the principle of Subsidiarity

First of all, the principle of Subsidiarity is of significance but also other provisions are of particular importance. The principle itself is not explicitly mentioned in the Convention, it was not the intention to take over the place of national human rights guarantees but to establish a supplementary instrument to the existing internal law. This pivotal idea is found in Article 60 ECHR, where it says 'Nothing in this Convention shall be construed as limiting or derogating from any of the human rights and fundamental freedoms which may be ensured under the laws of any High Contracting Party or under any other agreement to which it is a Party.'[124] Also Article 1 ECHR e.g. manifests this thought when it declares that the Member States shall secure the fundamental rights to each person within their jurisdiction. Further on, Article 13 ECHR requires the possibility to have access to an effective remedy before a national authority. Moreover, the form is not relevant e.g. '[...]does

[122] Case of Airey v. Ireland, judgment of 09.10.1979, ECHR.
[123] *Herbert Petzold* in Macdonald R.St.J., Matscher F. and Petzold H., *The european system for the protection of Human Rights* (1993), p. 41.
[124] see in appendix.

not go so far as to require any particular form of procedure; Contracting States are left a margin of domestic remedy for enforcement of a Convention Right.'[125]

Subsidiarity is also implied when the entitlement of the ECtHR dealt with a case only if an exhaustion of the domestic remedies is given. If it comes to the case that the authority is not a judicial authority, the given power is relevant. First of all, this conception implements the opportunity of each Member State to deal with the matters within their legal system and secondly, the accused State could solve the matter in good manner without being object of international interest. Further on, this mechanism is an internationally recognized by the rules of international law. The most significant effect is grounded in Article 26 ECHR, where it says 'The Commission may only deal with the matter after all domestic remedies have been exhausted, according to the generally recognized rules of international law, and within a period of six months from the date on which the final decision was taken.'[126] Article 57 ECHR states that there is a duty to respond to requests from the Council if it comes to questions whether or not the State offers an effective implementation of the guarantees. Obviously this means that the Council does have, although applying Article 1 ECHR, the power of monitoring.[127] 'The principle of Subsidiarity, as it applies within the framework of the European Convention on Human Rights, therefore refers primarily to the subsidiary role of the Convention machinery and entails first of all what may be termed a 'procedural relationship' between the national authorities responsible for implementing the Convention and deciding human-rights issues on the one hand and the Convention institutions on the other.[...]national authorities remained free to choose those measures which they considered appropriate in the matters governed by the Convention.'[128]

a. Further effects of the principle of Subsidiarity

However, the effect of the principle is much more widespread than thought at the first glance because it also means that the Court has to obey certain limits and is subjected to judicial self-restraint. The Court cannot undergo the competence of the national authorities if it comes to the case where the ECtHR has to decide upon an arbitrary distinction. Recognizing the principle of subsidiarity prompts the question which areas do have most conflict potential between the ECtHR and national authorities? Firstly, it needs to be clarified that the 'Strasbourg-machinery' is not a higher instance of controlling although in charge of monitoring the States. Nevertheless it does not

[125] *Herbert Petzold* in Macdonald R.St.J., Matscher F. and Petzold H., *The european system for the protection of Human Rights* (1993), p.45.

[126] see in Appendix.

[127] e.g.: *Herbert Petzold* in Macdonald R.St.J., Matscher F. and Petzold H., *The european system for the protection of Human Rights* (1993).

[128] *Herbert Petzold* in Macdonald R.St.J., Matscher F. and Petzold H., *The european system for the protection of Human Rights* (1993), p.49.

lead to the competence of revealing errors of national law. The situation is much more complex when national law is expressly mentioned or affected; therefore, this becomes an integral part of the Convention as in Articles 5 ECHR to 6 ECHR caused by their limited character and Articles 8 ECHR to 11 ECHR when constituting them as qualified rights, which means the Convention directly refers to domestic law. E.g. in the Prokopovich-case where it says 'The Court reiterates the Convention institutions' case-law that the concept of 'home' within the meaning of Article 8 ECHR is not limited to those which are lawfully occupied or which have been lawfully established. 'Home' is an autonomous concept that does not depend on classification under domestic law.'[129] In the light of the case-law the Court figured out that firstly it resides with the national authorities to apply domestic law and only in case of non-observance the Court examines a violation.[130]

Further on, an important matter of subsidiarity is when the right of the individual is dependent on the conduct of a national authority in charge. As a matter of fact the Court therefore not only decides whether lawfulness in terms of complying with e.g. procedural tasks of domestic law is given but also if arbitrariness has been avoided. This is best seen in Article 6 ECHR which guaran-

---

[129] Prokopovich v. Russia, judgment of 18.11.2004, ECHR.
This case was brought in by a Russian national who claimed to be violated in Article 8 of the Convention. The applicant and her partner together moved into an apartment provided by a State enterprise which happened to be the employer of the applicants partner. The couple never married but lived together as wife and husband. The applicant's partner died ten years later, thus she filed a request in order to be given an occupation certificate for the flat, which was refused. Thence, the claimant requested an investigation concerning the removal of her possessions and the eviction. The Court needed to decided how to define the term 'home' within the meaning of Article 8 by the reason of the fact that the flat was not legally established as her permanent residence. It noted that 'home' had to be seen as an autonomous concept which led to the effect that 'home' did not depend on a specific classification within the domestic law. In conclusion, the court held it necessary to prove the existence of a continuous and sufficient link with a certain place. If this link is provable, a specific place had to be classified as 'home', which was given in the applicant's case. Logically, an interference with Article 8 was concluded. Consequently, the Court questioned whether or not the given interference in form of an eviction was justifiable. Finally, The ECtHR decided that the eviction was not based on a court order nor did it sufficiently consider the established grounds by law. Therefore, a violation of Article 8 of the Convention was affirmed.

[130] e.g.: the impact of the principle of subsidiarity:
Reflection paper on the proposal to extend the court's advisory jurisdiction, http://echr.coe.int/Documents/Courts_advisory_jurisdiction_ENG.pdf, retrieved 25.08.2013.
e.g.: Letsas G., *A theory of Interpretation of the European Convention on Human Rights (*2007). http://fds.oup.com/www.oup.com/pdf/13/9780199203437.pdf, retrieved 25.08.2013.

X v. United Kingdom, judgment of 05.11.1981, ECHR.
The case was referred to the Court by the Commission of Human Rights after being lodged before the Commission. The applicant filed a complaint against the Broadmoor Hospital (a special secure mental hospital) on the ground of a unjustified re-detention. Further, he noted that he had no effective measures of challenging the re-detention. The Mental health Act 1959 stated, firstly, if a convicted person suffered from mental illness (e.g.: psychopathic disorder, subnormality, mental disorders) and, secondly, if the person concerned posed a severe threat to the public, the Court was allowed to make a further restriction order. The applicant was diagnosed with paranoid psychosis. However, his wife claimed to the probation officer in charge that the plaintiff's conditions got worse. According to the applicant, no further detailed information concerning his detention (re-call) were given by the police nor by the hospital authorities. By that reasons, he claimed that Article 5 was violated. Para 4 of article 5 was violated by the fact that the claimant could not make effective and immediate use of his rights if not being adequately and promptly informed about the reasons of the re-call. On the other hand, the ECtHR clearly stated that the claimant did not suffer from a breach of para 1 due to the circumstance that the decisive medical judgment was objective and reliable. Therefore, the Court held that there was a breach of Article 5 (4) but no breach of Article 5(1).

tees a fair trial to everyone. '[...]the admissibility of evidence is primarily governed by domestic law [...] Only exceptional circumstances could prompt the European Court to conclude that the failure to hear a person as a witness was incompatible with the Convention.'[131]

Another important role can be revealed within rights which need regulatory national conducting. Those are limited rights as mentioned above, those which are subjected to restrictions or conditions as well as those which require regulations or positive actions set by the Member States. To deal adequately with these matters the Court developed and acknowledged the instrument of the margin of appreciation, which mostly is indicated by words like 'wide', 'certain' etc. Although accepting the States democratic systems, ruling and background the Court has the final saying. Also the domestic authorities bring the principle the full meaning when implementing the provisions of the Convention in a wide spread sense. ' In the exercise of their supervisory function, the Convention institutions cannot disregard the legal and factual features characterizing the life of society in the respondent State.'[132]

B. The Interpretation of the Convention

1. Methods developed and utilized by the European Court of Human Rights

By the end of 2012, the ECtHR's statistic elaborated that according to their general statistical information 65.150 applications were allocated to a judicial formation. In 1.678 cases a judgment was delivered, in 86.201 cases were struck out or declared inadmissible.[133] These facts demonstrate the mass of cases the ECtHR has to deal with, in respect of the quite brief time of its existence. Not only is the amount of applications is significant but also the endowment of the more or less abstract 'termini' of the ECHR which the Court developed through case law. In the following analyze, the different ways of interpretive methods and the work of the Court will be revealed regarding its casuistic case-law which only has capability of being generalized by relatively little occasions. This is a consequence of judicial self-restraint and an emanation of the fact that legal doctrine is much less important than it happens to be within national law. Those circumstances find its source in the limitlessly varying legal systems where the cases originate from. Although it is not immediately obvious the Court uses empirical methods in order to answer specific questions and if an accumulation of such specific cases is affirmed the organs attempt to formulate generally valid statements. When interpreting international matters firstly it needs to be referred to the Articles 31 to 33 of the

---

[131] *Herbert Petzold* in Macdonald R.St.J., Matscher F. and Petzold H., *The european system for the protection of Human Rights* (1993), p.54.

[132] *Herbert Petzold* in Macdonald R.St.J., Matscher F. and Petzold H., *The european system for the protection of Human Rights* (1993), p. 58.

[133] http://www.echr.coe.int/Documents/Stats_analysis_2012_ENG.pdf retrieved 26.08.2013.

Vienna Convention on the Law of Treaties of 1969.[134] '[...] on the Law of Treaties gave expression to generally accepted principles of international law on the interpretation of treaties between nations, so that the Court should too by them interpreting the Convention.'[135] Clearly this implements the obligation to admit that the text regarding its objects and purposes needs to be seen as the main starting point of an interpretation. Regarding the ECHR, the preamble offers the starting point when it says 'the realization of fundamental rights' but also the 'Travaux Préparatoires' offer a supplementation.[136]

In the following chapters the methods, which were developed and recognized, but also criticized, will be illustrated; hence a better understanding of the chain of thoughts and argumentation of the ECtHR can be provided.

a. The evolutive interpretation

'As regards their belief that judicial corporal punishment deters criminals, it must be pointed out that a punishment does not lose its degrading character just because it is believed to be, or actually is, an effective deterrent or aid to crime control. Above all, as the Court must emphasize, it is never permissible to have recourse to punishments which are contrary to Article 3 ECHR, whatever their deterrent effect may be. The Court must also recall that the Convention is a living instrument which, as the Commission rightly stressed, must be interpreted in the light of present-day conditions. In the case the Court cannot but be influenced by the developments and commonly accepted standards in the penal policy of the Member States of the Council of Europe in this field.'[137] Indeed, the Attorney-General for the Isle of Man mentioned that, for many years, the provisions of Manx legislation concerning judicial corporal punishment had been under review.'[138] The Tyrer judgment was called a landmark case because of its obvious referral to the obligation of the Court to interpret

---

[134] http://untreaty.un.org/ilc/texts/instruments/english/conventions/1_1_1969.pdf, retrieved 25.08.2013.

[135] Matscher F. in Macdonald R.St.J., Matscher F. and Petzold H., *The european system for the protection of Human Rights* (1993), p. 65.

[136] e.g.: Matscher F. in Macdonald R.St.J., Matscher F. and Petzold H., *The european system for the protection of Human Rights* (1993).

[137] e.g.: Tyrer v. the United Kingdom, judgment of 25.04.1978, ECHR.

[138] Tyrer v. the United Kingdom, judgment of 25.04.1978, para. 31, ECHR.

The claimant Tyrer, a citizen of the United Kingdom, was a resident of the Isle of Man. The Isle of Man was part of the United Kingdom but had its own administrative and legal system. At the age of 15 he pleaded guilty to unlawful assault in form of bodily harming to an other pupil at his school. Therefore, the applicant was sentenced to three strokes of the birch according to the law. Concerning the international law, the United Kingdom found that international treaties should be extended to such territories as the Isle of Man. Although withdrawing the application by the claimant, the Commission found that general questions arose which evidently are of major importance, hence, the case was not stroke out of the list. By that reason, the Court had to clarify whether or not a breach of Article 3 was committed. The Court found that Tyrer did not suffer from such a punishment so that it could be spoken of torture, nor could be spoken of inhuman punishment within the meaning of Article 3. According to the Court further criterion, for example, all circumstances, the nature and context of the punishment, the methods, etc, must be interpreted in order to speak of the terms 'degrading' or 'inhuman'. Moreover, the Court explicitly stated that the Convention had to be interpreted in the light of the present day conditions. Finally, the Court held that the punishment, in regard of the entire circumstances, was humiliating and attained the level inherent to a 'degrading punishment'.

the Convention in respect of the social development and territorial circumstances. One could say that the Convention is open to a dynamic interpretation and its desirable vice to the historical state of society to specify terminologies. To clarify that, it can be referred to the preamble of the ECHR and also to the Statutes of the Council where it says that the purposes have to be realized, which imply the imperative conclusion to do so in an evolutive modality.[139]

aa. The application of the evolutive interpretation within the case-law of the ECtHR

When deepening the thought of evolutive interpretation the boundary of acting within a legislative field approximates abruptly which has to be reflected judiciously. 'It cannot be the task of the interpreter to change the content of a norm; but if the content of a norm undergo a change of social reality, the interpreter must take account of this.'[140] To make this theoretical aspect more obvious and transparent, specific chosen cases will be analyzed at this juncture.

(1) The case of Rees v. the UK

In 1986, the Court initially had to confront itself with the issue of gender identity changes. The claimant, in the case, was with all physical and biological characteristics born female person, at the time of birth.[141] In 1971 after hormonal treatment she changed her name to Brendan Mark Rees. Thus he requested a new passport but in regard of his original gender the prefix Mr. was refused. Several attempts to persuade the Parliament so that they concern themselves to resolve the problematic of transsexuality in the given perspective remained unsuccessful until 1984. As to the law of the United Kingdom the change of name is possible without further noteworthy restrictions and if a civil status certificate is needed which actually can be in form of a driving license the prefix is adopted to the appropriate gender also in case of transsexuality. Birth certificates reveal historical facts concerning an individual which means that the birth certificate order constitutes propriety and authentication of evidence. The determination of the sex has to be followed by the rules of the 1953 Act which only recognizes the biological criteria, chromosomal, gonadal and genital sex but the psychological sex is not considered. Logically a change of the first record caused by error of determination of the sex has to be refused.[142] Furthermore, the record is prima facie evidence the matter arises again when it comes to the issue of marriage concerning the fact that only two individuals of the opposite sex can be married. The required records include the birth certificate. A few other cases regarding the definition of the sex were cited where it says e.g. 'In one case

[139] e.g.: Matscher F. in Macdonald R.St.J., Matscher F. and Petzold H., *The european system for the protection of Human Rights* (1993).
[140] *Diritto internazionale I* (1956), p.182 cited by Matscher F. in Macdonald R.St.J., Matscher F. and Petzold H., *The european system for the protection of Human Rights* (1993), p.70.
[141] Rees v. The United Kingdom, judgment of 17.10.1986. para. 12, ECHR.
[142] Rees v. the United Kingdom, judgment of 17.10.1986, ECHR.

concerning prostitution, a male to female transsexual, who had undergone both hormone and surgical treatment, was nevertheless treated as a male by the Court of Appeal for the purposes of Section 30 of the Sexual Offences Act 1956 and Section 5 of the Sexual Offences Act 1967.'[143]

The applicant alleged a violation of respecting private life of individuals enshrined in Article 8 of the Convention. '[...] constraints upon his full integration into social life which were a result of the failure of the Government to provide measures that would legally constitute him as a male[...]. In particular, he complained of the practice of issuing him with a birth certificate on which his sex continued to be recorded as "female". [...]'[144] Primarily, the intent of Article 8 ECHR is to protect the individual in case of indiscriminate interference of national authorities. The crux of the concerned case is whether the existence of positive obligations of States is recognized or not. Should the British Government modify the available system because of the respect of privacy in terms of private life urgently demands such a positive legal action? The Commission held that the applicant was socially fully accepted as man and, therefore, the recognition should be given by the UK. The decision of the Court based on the argumentation that a recognition is given by the fact that transsexuals can change their names and receive the preferred prefix.[145]

Further on, the demands are satisfied in relation to the extent of the legal system. The core of such concepts needs to be the balance between individuals and the generally formulated interests of a wider community on the opposite. The question whether a system needs to offer provisions for civil status certificates has to be denied although the Commission held it unjustified that the historical sexual identity handicaps individuals e.g. regarding marriage, retirement. Changing the record of birth register in such cases would undergo the legitimate interest of others in terms of information about the true facts and the legal significance would be questioned. Regarding the demand to exclude third parties of receiving such information the Court laid down the fact that this may result in a prejudice of purposes. '[...] it must for the time being left to the respondent State to determine to what extent it can meet the remaining demands of transsexuals. However, the Court is conscious of the seriousness of the problems affecting these persons and the distress they suffer. The Convention has always to be interpreted and applied in the light of current circumstances.'[146] Conclusive there is no violation of Article 8 ECHR nor of Article 12 ECHR.

---

143 Rees v. the United Kingdom, judgment of 17.10.1986, para. 29, ECHR.
144 Rees v. the United Kingdom, judgment of 17.10.1986, para. 34, ECHR.
145 Rees v. the United Kingdom, judgment of 17.10.1986, ECHR.
146 Rees v. the United Kingdom, judgment of 17.10.1986, para. 47, ECHR.

(2) The case of Cossey v. the UK

This case was brought up ten years after the Rees-case and it did not vary much besides the different demands.[147] The applicant was registered as a person of the male sex. After undergoing several treatments and surgeries Cossey fully lived as a female person according to the medical reports. The claimant wanted to enter into marriage. In the UK entering a marriage is possible if not being of the same sex. 'In English law, marriage is defined as a voluntary union for life of one man and one woman to the exclusion of all others'.[148] This claim was denied by authorities because of the fact that her birth certificate substantiated her of male sex and a proposal of changing the records was rejected based on similar arguments as in the Rees-case. The Court argued that if not denying the instrument of marriage consequently would have been void. The fact that in the concerning case a relationship is given and the will of both to enter the marriage does not make it material distinguishable from the Rees-case. At that point it clearly is debatable if the Court would have had to reconsider its further judgment especially regarding the definition of the term interference. The Commission and the claimant argued that 'Nevertheless, this would not prevent the Court from departing from an earlier decision if it was persuaded that there were cogent reasons for doing so. Such a departure might, for example, be warranted in order to ensure that the interpretation of the Convention reflects societal changes and remains in line with present-day conditions.'[149] Does the refusal of changing the birth record imply an interference with the respect of private life? The Court repeated itself when defending the 'Rees-argumentation', birth records require historical facts in order to guarantee a proper documentation, an annotation to the records would only establish that belonging to the other sex, but not from the time of birth, the annotation would be public otherwise a fundamental modification of the nature of birth registers would be demanded. Ergo, the Court decided concerning Article 8 ECHR 'refusal to alter the register of births or to issue birth certificates whose contents and nature differ from those of the original entries cannot be considered as an interference with her respect for private life.'[150] Inter alia, those arguments were similar to the Rees-case and significant that, although ten years later, the Court is still persisting on the same point of view regarding the public character of such a record, its effects. Of significant importance, debatable of course, is the Court's definition of interference which, if denying, consequently leads to a refusal of positives obligations. Also the Court repeated that legal measures have to be complemented in regard to societal and scientific variances, which by that time, according to the Court did not take place although certain members harmonized their common law in that specific field. This

[147] Cossey v. the United Kingdom, judgment of 27.09.1990, ECHR.
[148] Cossey v. the United Kingdom, judgment of 27.09.1990, para. 23, ECHR.
[149] Cossey v. the United Kingdom, judgment of 27.09.1990, para. 35, ECHR.
[150] Cossey v. the United Kingdom, judgment of 27.09.1990, ECHR.

among other reasons may be referred to the Recommendation 1117 of the Assembly in 1989.[151] Finally, there is not enough common ground to reconsider the argumentation according to the Court. Regarding a violation of Article 12 ECHR the Court noted that firstly the right to marriage is limited and secondly that such a restriction does not need to be in an extent so that its essential core would be impaired. The obstacle to marry cannot be found on the part of the national law and its limitations because they are protecting the traditional marriage otherwise the concept would be abandoned.[152]

(3) Judicial re-consideration of the former judgments: The case of Christine Goodwin v. the UK

The applicant is a male to female transsexual by gender re-assignment surgery. Between 1990 to 1992 she complained of sexual harassment at her work but before the Industrial Tribunal she was unsuccessful caused by the fact that formally according to the law she was seen as male. Starting at a new company she was requested to provide her National Insurance number. Afterwards she experienced continual problems with her colleagues. She was informed by the DDS Contributions Agency that her work had to be continued until reaching the age of 65 which is the age of retirement of men. The consequences were much more drastic, as she claimed; if any provisions were offered for women by the Government she could not receive them or attend because she was obeyed to wait until the age of a male person because of her birth record, regarding insurances, mortgages or even private pensions the claimant had to pay the same amount as a person of male sex.[153] 'The applicant argued that rapid changes, in respect of the scientific understanding of, and the social attitude towards, transsexualism were taking place not only across Europe but elsewhere.' On the other hand the Government argued that 'Referring to the Court's case-law, the Government maintained that there was no generally accepted approach among the Contracting States in respect of transsexuality and that, in view of the margin of appreciation left to States under the Convention, the lack of recognition in the United Kingdom of the applicant's new gender identity for legal purposes did not entail a violation of Article 8 of the Convention.'[154]

Regarding the 'DDS-issues' it held that the policy of confidentiality is assured and besides the claimant had been issued with a total new ID. As a result of the system the DDS was applying employees are not under any circumstances able to achieve further intimate information about the

---

[151] Reports have been made; and caused by that, an adoption of resolutions by the European Parliament took place in 1989, which were adopted by the Parliamentary Assembly of the Council of Europe in the same year.
Recommendation 1117 (1989) of the Council of Europe on the conditions of transsexuals.
[152] Cossey v. the United Kingdom, judgment of 27.09.1990, ECHR.
[153] Christine Goodwin v. the United Kingdom, judgment of 11.07.2002, ECHR.
[154] Christine Goodwin v. the United Kingdom, judgment of 11.07.2002, para. 63 to 64, ECHR.

holder. The matter of retirement has to be regarded within the European point of view and systematical denouement which is proved in the UK. As mentioned before, the claimant unsuccessfully complained harassment at work, she could have pressed charges through applying criminal law, in specific, the Sex discrimination Act 1975. As to the argumentation of the Court, it did considerate whether or not the positive obligation of ensuring to respect the private life through legal recognition is sufficiently implemented while applying the margin of appreciation. The consideration is influenced by the diversity of each case.[155] It laid down that within the legal perspective the claimant remains as a male person. This leads to the effect that sex related regulations are applicable, inter alia, in the fields of entitlements, insurances etc.

Finally, it cannot be regarded as a minor inconvenience, much more likely as an interference, if aspects of personal identity contravene with insufficient legally clarified domestic law. 'The coherence of the administrative and legal practices, within the domestic system, must be regarded as an important factor in the assessment carried out under Article 8 of the Convention.'[156]

If a State provides gender re-assignment surgery, on the one hand, it would be illogical to deny the implication of the result of such an operation within the legal sphere. Further on, it noted that as justification in order to continue the concerned governmental handling aspects of scientific nature were slight superficial but in fact the medical consideration itself clearly cannot be the main foundation for a legal recognition. 'In accordance with the principle of subsidiarity, it is indeed primarily for the Contracting States to decide on the measures necessary to secure Convention rights within their jurisdiction and, in resolving within their domestic legal systems the practical problems created by the legal recognition of post-operative gender status, the Contracting States must enjoy a wide margin of appreciation.'[157] Although respecting the principles it did emphasis that probably a common ground is not yet developed but this fact does not quasi justify the non-recognition.[158] Further, the Court clarified that the circumstances in which post-operative transsexu-

---

[155] e.g.: The core of the reflection of the Court finds the same approach as in the Cossey-case.

[156] Christine Goodwin v. the United Kingdom, judgment of 17.09.2002, para. 78, ECHR.

[157] Christine Goodwin v. the United Kingdom, judgment of 17.09.2002, para. 85, ECHR.

[158] e.g.: Sheffield and Horsham v. the United Kingdom, judgment of 30.07.1998, ECHR.

In this case the Court found that there was no breach of Article 8, nor of Article 12 of the Convention. The main question was whether or not the respondent State was the addressee of a positive obligation to recognize the changed sexual identity of the claimant, after undergoing medical surgery (post-operative transsexual by gender reassignment). The first applicant was born and registered as being of the male sex. The claimant complained, being the target of discrimination at work, further, that her employer dismissed her as pilot after undergoing the gender re-assignment. Consequently, she attributed the fact that obtaining employment seemed impossible in large parts to the legal position of transsexuals within the United Kingdom. The second claimant, Mrs. Horsham, acquired Netherlands citizenship after naturalization. She was registered as being of the male sex. She was issued a birth certificate by the Registrar in The Hague recording that she was of the female sex. Hence, she requested that the original birth certificate in the United Kingdom be changed in order to record her new sex. Instead of amending the certificate the Office of Population Census and Surveys declared it to be impossible by the reason of the non-existence of any such provision. The claimant filed a complaint stating that by that circumstances she was forced to stay abroad, and besides, that she was precluded from entering into marriage. The Court reiterated the decision and

als are living is no longer sustainable and a fair balance has to be established, when the Court says 'the Court considers that society may reasonably be expected to tolerate a certain inconvenience to enable individuals to live in dignity and worth in accordance with the sexual identity chosen by them at great personal cost.'[159] In result of the further explained circumstances and investigated under the light of a developing, in terms of changing, society a violation of Article 8 ECHR had been observed. Regarding the accused violation of Article 12 ECHR the arguments of the Court found its base on the consideration that it is no more sustainable to take the factor of biological congruence only in order to justify the non-recognition. The society drastically changed, hence consequently caused by the nature of the ECHR as a living instrument, the interpretation of marriage urgently has to be reconsidered and newly defined. Although her right to marry was not infringed because she obviously could have entered marriage but only to a person of the opposite of her former sex, the question remains: 'Can there be any breach of the concerned right although she was remaining able to marry ?' In 2001, the Court clearly declared that no instrument could possibly offer justification to exclude transsexuals from marrying a person, who formally would be the same sex. Principles of interpretation cannot be utilized so that in conclusion the exercise of rights suffers from an effective bar. Of course, it is the obligation of the legal authorities to specify and to accomplish basis, but the condition must be justified in the light of the present day and cannot contravene the process of seeking human rights law related interpretations. Therefore, a breach of Article 12 ECHR is given.[160]

b. The margin of appreciation

The Convention organs when being actors in judgments, opinions or recommendations have the compulsory responsibility to act respecting the cultural, historical, social, ideological and legal conditions within the Member States because homogeneity and streamlining is not dictated. Although certain boundaries are logically given; otherwise the Europeanization reduces itself to absurdity. An enormous amount of cases expressly revealed inevitable legal circumstances e.g. 'the sense of common law, the life sentence, the contempt of Court, the insertion of administrative proceedings or disciplinary proceedings before professional bodies as a preliminary to Court decision in certain civil and criminal cases,[...].'[161]

---

argumentation of the Cossey as well as the Rees case. Although several years passed since then, the ECtHR found that there was no common ground within the Member States. Re-assignment surgeries and the 'phenomenon' of transsexuals were still controversial and critical regarding the moral, scientific, societal aspects. Despite these statements, the Court stated that it was of high importance to develop appropriate legal measures but that a positive obligation of the State could not be inflicted.

[159] Christine Goodwin v. the United Kingdom, judgment of 17.09.2001, para. 91, ECHR.

[160] Christine Goodwin v. the United Kingdom, judgment of 17.09.2001, ECHR.

[161] Matscher F. in *The European System for the Protection of Human Rights (*1993), p.75.

aa. Theoretical aspects of the margin of appreciation

Obviously the margin of appreciation is sensitive in order to establish a continual balance between the sovereignty of the Members and the provisions which must to be kept in respect of a certain amount of discretion.[162] Primarily this instrument takes effect when adjudicating in the field of Articles 8, 9, 10, 11, 14, 15 as well as Article 1 of Protocol No.1 of the Convention. Interestingly this is also utilized when it comes to the issue of positive obligations, inter alia, in the Goodwin-case. MacDonald R.St.J. put it that way 'The fact is that variations in the width different rights, different claims in respect of the same right by applicants in different situations, and with different justifications advanced by States at different times.'[163]

Since the existence of the ECHR the margin of appreciation became more and more unalterable due to the increasing developments and changes within Europe. The ECtHR has to be said as a supervisory functionary respectively reviewing the conformity of standards and consequently, if the case is given, offering appropriate remedies. The point of 'acting accurate and offering legal appropriateness' in case of a declination of a further 'remedy' can only lead to one of two conclusions, the first is that the substitution of the domestic courts' decision would be inappropriate, regarding a particular issue. Secondly, that the ECtHR reviewed the matter in specific but finds the argumentation to be appropriate and justifiable. In reality, the distinction between the two of them can easily be obscured by utilizing the margin of appreciation when the instrument itself prevents the reasoning of the Court in case of non-intervention in the national courts' 'arbitration'. If the Court does so the instrument constitutes the argumentation but the material argumentation behind is invisible which enshrines the matter in a particular unclarity. To put it into one phrase: the margin of appreciation simply is the drawback of the sovereignty.[164]

bb. Analyzes of the case law in respect of the margin of appreciation

At this juncture analyzes of several cases will reveal the dimensions and the scope of this specific principle in detail. In order to offer an accurate and clear exposition of the mentioned principle, the following cases will mainly be discussed in the light of an accused violation of the right of the freedom of expression.

---

[162] Hilson C., *Global Constitutionalism - The margin of appreciation, domestic irregularity and domestic court rulings in ECHR environmental jurisprudence: Global legal pluralism in action*, Vol. 2, p. 265, CLJ (2013).
[163] MacDonald R.St.J. in *The European System for the Protection of Human Rights* (1993), p. 84.
[164] e.g.: *The European System for the Protection of Human Rights* (1993).
Emmerson B., Ashworth A.,Macdonald A., *Human Rights and Criminal Justice* (2012).

(1) The case of the Sunday Times v. the UK in the light of Article 10 ECHR

α) The facts

Thalidomide is a drug which was manufactured and marketed by Distillers Company; under license in the United Kingdom. The drug contained an ingredient, initially developed in the Federal Republic of Germany. After using the drug during the pregnancy, several women gave birth to children who were suffering from severe deformities.[165] A number of writs of affected parents were issued but the negotiated cases never proceeded to trial. The publisher of a weekly newspaper, the Sunday Times, began to do serious investigation and acquired a whole range of articles concerning the negligent acting of Distillers, the further scientific opinions and the desperate situation of the parents in order to gain an adequate and more generous settlement. One specific Article dealt with the procedures of marketing, former testings in Germany and its results, the lack of sufficient testing by Distillers, etc. The Article has not been published by the time the Attorney-General obtained an injunction inhibiting the publication. The reasoning of the Attorney-General concerned the contempt of the Court. It stated that justice would probably be denied because the case would be affected if it comes to a publication. In the particular case, all the circumstances led to the conclusion that a severe risk of an interference had been given, hence the course of justice would have been endangered. Further, the Court noted that there was no public interest in an immediate disclosure of the case details. It concluded that the pressure, which the parties of the litigation would have to face, did not overweigh the public interests. Moreover, the Court found that the freedom of action of Distiller´s regarding the litigation clearly would be affected in a negative way, and therefore obviously lead to a contempt. The Court of Appeal did rescind the injunction. The House of Lords restored the injunction arguing similar as the Attorney-General.[166]

β) Examination of a violation of Article 10 of the ECHR

The issue, which had to be considered before the ECtHR was whether or not there had been a violation caused by interference, by the authorities which did not satisfy the requirements of exceptional matters. The Court held that 'It is clear that there was an 'interference by public authority' in the exercise of the applicants' freedom of expression, which is guaranteed by paragraph 1 of Article 10 [...]. Such an interference entails a 'violation' of Article 10 [...] if it does not fall within one of the exceptions provided for in paragraph 2[...]. The Court therefore has to examine in turn whether the interference in the present case was 'prescribed by law', whether it had

[165] Sunday Times v. the United Kingdom, judgment of 26.04.1979, para. 8, ECHR.
[166] Sunday Times v. the United Kingdom, judgment of 26.04.1979, ECHR.

an aim or aims that is or are legitimate under Article 10 (2) [...] and whether it was 'necessary in a democratic society' for the aforesaid aim or aims.'[167]

γ) The argumentation of the ECtHR

The arguments were as following, the Court clarified that ensuring freedom of expression is one of the fundamental mechanisms within a democratic society. If information is e.g. offensive, indifferently or disturbing it is not applicable under the light of subparagraph two. Further on it does not matter whether the information provided is press related or refers to the administration of justice. If information is provided why shouldn't there be a forum of discussion besides the Courts'? 'Not only do the media have the task of imparting such information[...]:the public also has a right to receive them.'[168] Consequently, the Court found that there was an interference with the freedom of expression. Logical consequence was to weight up the diverting interests in form of deciding whether or not the interference could be justified. This chain of thought implies that the mechanism of a margin of appreciation found utilization when stating that in regard of the sovereignty the authorities are in legal position to interfere with fundamental rights on the one hand but on the other hand the Court examined whether that particular infringement finds justification in accordance with the Convention under the light of a European understanding and definition. The case was called a landmark because the Court held that the violation cannot be justified; it was not convinced from the explanation by the national authorities. 'That restraint proves not to be proportionate to the legitimate aim pursued; it was not necessary in a democratic society for maintaining the authority of the judiciary.'[169]

δ) Conclusion

It was astonishing that the ECtHR applied the margin of appreciation and concluded in its review that there is no justifiable argument regarding the urgent need of the democratic society. As it will be revealed later, several judgments showed the sign of the fact the the margin of appreciation is used often, especially when it comes to 'difficult to take side' or political issues where the ECtHR seems to be tempted to utilize a wide narrow of margin of appreciation or is that presumption solely a melodramatic assumption? In accordance to the primarily point of view e.g. F.A. Mann stated 'the standards and traditions of English law and English public life it is the decision of the House of Lords or that of the European Court of Human Rights which more correctly assesses the 'social need' and 'legitimate aim' of a civilized society[...].'[170] Other authors assumed that this decision

---

[167] Sunday TImes v. the United Kingdom, judgment of 26.04.1979, para. 46, ECHR.
[168] Janis M., Kay R., Bradley A., *European Human Rights Law* (2008), *p.83.*
[169] Sunday TImes v. the United Kingdom, judgment of 26.04.1979, para. 67, ECHR.
[170] Janis M., Kay R., Bradley A., *European Human Rights Law* (2008), *p.86.*

could be a serious challenge for the States e.g. Gray Christine noted too that the decision forces to reconsider the national behavior; 'Perhaps this case will remind English courts of the potentially embarrassing consequence of ignoring the existence of the European Convention on Human Rights and encourage them in a more constructive approach to its application.'[171] Apparently the decision had its impact on both of them.

(2) The case of Handyside v. the UK regarding the freedom of speech

α) The facts

This case firstly recognized the importance of the freedom of speech. [172] The claimant published the little red schoolbook which freely circulated within several European countries at that time. The booklet contained, inter alia: 'All grown-ups are paper tigers', an 'Introduction to the British edition', and chapters on the following subjects: Education, Learning, Teachers, Pupils and The System. The chapter on Pupils contained a twenty-six page section concerning 'Sex' which included the following sub-sections: Masturbation, Orgasm, Intercourse and petting, Contraceptives, Wet dreams, Menstruation, Child-molesters or 'dirty old men', Pornography, Impotence, Homosexuality, Normal and abnormal, Find out more, Venereal diseases, Abortion, Legal and illegal abortion, Remember, Methods of abortion, Addresses for help and advice on sexual matters.'[173] After publishing action took place against the release of the book on the ground of Obscene Publications Act 1959 in conjunction with the Obscene Publications Act 1964, which manifests that an act is obscene when it affects people who are likely having regard to all circumstances with depravation. Such a publication can be justified if conducing for the common public good. The Court found that the book emphasizes only on specific matters while not having a balanced content, e.g. the institution of marriage is not mentioned at all. This possibly contravenes the educational perspective of children with religious background, the illegality of consumption of pot is not brought up, furthermore, the illegality of sexual intercourse before a particular age, etc. Therefore, it concluded that the publication indeed was obscene.[174]

---

e.g.: Loveland I., *Constitutional Law, Administrative Law and Human Rights: A critical introduction (2012)*, p. 606.

[171] Gray C., *European Convention on Human Rights - Freedom of Expression and the Thalidomide Case,* The Cambridge Law Journal/Volume 38, November 1979, pp. 242 to 245.

[172] Handyside v. the United Kingdom, judgment of 07.12.1976, ECHR.

[173] Handyside v. the United Kingdom, judgment of 07.12.1976, para. 20, ECHR.

[174] Handyside v. the United Kingdom, judgment of 07.12.1976, ECHR.

β) The argumentation offered by the different entities

Although affirming an obscenity the Court did not deny the fact that in regard of all the circumstances and disadvantages the claimant had to suffer an interference took place and only could be justified if the public authorities acted in accordance with subparagraph two of Article 10 ECHR.[175] 'According to the Government and the majority of the Commission, the interferences were 'necessary in a democratic society', 'for the protection of ... morals'.'[176] This is where the Court referred to the margin of appreciation. It stated that in first place it is the responsibility of each Member State to offer sufficient protection of fundamental rights and the established mechanisms of the Court have to be utilized subsidiary. It seems to be impossible to formulate a general valid definition of 'what are defensible morals?'. The Court held that 'The view taken by their respective laws of the requirements of morals varies from time to time and from place to place, especially in our era which is characterized by a rapid and far-reaching evolution of opinions on the subject.'[177] This consequently means that morals are valued as elastic and divergently defined issues and logically the term 'social need' also is variable in the specific case. The authorities itself have to define the necessity of the protection of morals for the common societal good. Nevertheless, the Court appreciates the margin of appreciation but do state that this cannot lead to unlimited power and the Court puts itself in the position of reviewing the domestic decision, in fact being a supervisor. In conclusion, although not entirely supporting the domestic Courts argumentation, the ECtHR held that no violation of Article 10 ECHR is given; 'the national margin of appreciation and the optional nature of the 'restrictions' and 'penalties' referred to in Article 10 (2) prevent the Court from accepting the argument. The Contracting States have each fashioned their approach in the light of the situation obtaining in their respective territories; they have had regard, inter alia, to the different views prevailing there about the demands of the protection of morals in a democratic society.'[178]

δ) Conclusion and further consequences of the judgment

In the judgment the focus laid on divergent issues, the first one was whether or not the ECtHR should stay in the position of being a supervisor, hence utilizing the margin of appreciation because of the lack of common ground within Europe. This means that the respondent State remained in charge of defining the concerned terms, only in case of an unnecessary interference and a much higher common harmonization within the Member States in accordance with the Convention the Court would probably have held a violation. As already revealed, the Court found that there has been an interference of the claimants' right. Secondly, the question has to be answered whether or

---

[175] e.g.: Janis M.W., Kay R.S., Bradley A.W., *European human Rights Law* (2008), p.239.
[176] Handyside v. the United Kingdom, judgment of 07.12.1976, para. 45, ECHR.
[177] Handyside v. the United Kingdom, judgment of 07.12.1978, ECHR.
[178] Janis M.W., Kay R.S., Bradley A.W., *European human Rights Law* (2008), p.241.

not that interference is necessary in order to protect domestic values. Was it necessary at that time amongst the UKs' democratic society to interfere with such sanctions and disadvantages for the claimant in order to achieve certain morals? At first appearance this might not seem to have a deeper impact but the contrary is the case. It solely depends on the opinion of the ECtHR as to whether or not such necessity is given by applying a narrower, or alternatively a less narrow margin. The wider the margin the less realistic is a successful complaint is. In 1988, the Court tried to establish a sort of test mechanism e.g. within the Olsson-case when stating that 'In essence the question is whether the national court has misjudged the necessity. The Government favored the minority's approach, adding that a wide margin of appreciation should be afforded to the national authorities so long as there was no reason to believe that the decisions were not taken in good faith, with due care and in a reasonable manner. The approach which the Court has consistently adopted - and from which it sees no reason to depart on the present occasion - differs somewhat from those described above. In the first place, its review is not limited to ascertaining whether a respondent State exercised its discretion reasonably, carefully and in good faith [...] must look at them in the light of the case as a whole; it must determine whether the reasons adduced to justify the interferences at issue are 'relevant and sufficient'.[179]

In the former case the Court utilized quite a wide narrow when stating that each Member has to decide for its own good how to protect the morals best in order to satisfy the democratic functioning and development of the society. Further presumptions can be made in the case, firstly, is it the primarily function of the freedom of speech to be dependent on the accused States' definition when interference has occur and when giving the accused contracting party the ability to profit from a wide margin can freedoms best be protected? As a consequent thought one would have to deny that

---

[179] Olsson v. Sweden, judgment of 24.03.1988, para. 67, ECHR.
The claimants were parents of the three children concerned. The parents spent some time at a home for the mentally retarded, respectively. Different social authorities were involved within the family business prior the questioned advents. The children should be taken into care by the reason that the parents were seen to be unable to satisfy the children's needs. In specific, the children were considerably retarded and urgently needed special treatment. At all time, the parents did not sufficiently cooperated with the authorities or the institutions in charge, further, they denied being mentally retarded and therefore, not capable of taking satisfactory care of the three children. According to the Swedish child-welfare legislation measures had to be taken in order to guarantee the favorable development of children which, inter alia, could lead to stay in a foster home or similar institution. Under an other Act, the compulsory care had to be terminated if the targeted aim was achieved and the measures were not necessary anymore. Mr. and Mrs. Olsson, inter alia, alleged a violation of Article 8 by the reasons of the care decision and the following replacement of the children. The fact that the children were taken into public care was seen as an interference with the right to respect the family life, consequently, the question was if the interference concerned were in accordance with the law and, further, if so, were they necessary within a democratic society. The term 'in accordance with the law' not only required specific compatibility with the domestic law, but also a certain quality of the law. A law which interfered with the provisions of the Convention, thus needed to be foreseeable. The applied swedish law was not general in terms and provided actual intervention in case of a jeopardized life/health of a child. The Court held that the purposes concerned were acceptable and reasonable, consequently, the aim was legitimate. Regarding the necessity of the administrative acting was considered not to be proportionate, although the Court took into account that a margin of appreciation was left to the Members. In conclusion, the Court found that there was a breach of Article 8 by the reason of implementing such a care decision, but not the decision itself.

because the necessity will vary within the divergent measures of each Member State, but the Court held that the Members itself are best to achieve the aim because of their connection to the vital forces.[180]

But are such widely divergent States able to guarantee a constant protection? A drastic limitation of the freedom of speech can occur within the margin of appreciation which could lead to the question whether or not the utilization of the margin of appreciation insidiously dilutes the protected freedoms?

dd. The difficulties regarding the utilization of an the margin of appreciation

As shown above, the margin of appreciation practically is a complex instrument which met with opposition; critics reproach that the ECtHR utilizes a much too wide margin in cases where it actually should be a much more narrower one in order to abolish circumvention of the provisioned rights by the States' authorities. By the examples of further case analyzes the problematic of utilizing the adequate margin of appreciation shall be illustrated.

(1) The case of Hirst v. the UK

α) The facts

In respect of the right to vote, which is established through Article 3 ECHR, the first case and its dissenting opinions and criticism shall give an insight to understand the difficulty of applying the margin of appreciation. Regarding the concerned case the facts were: On the ground of diminished responsibility the claimant was found guilty to manslaughter. His guilty plea was accepted based on medical evidence that he was a man with a severe personality disorder to such a degree that he was amoral. Consequently he had to face a term of discretionary life imprisonment. The applicant's tariff (that part of the sentence relating to retribution and deterrence) expired on 25 June 1994.'[181] The applicant demanded to have the right to vote but under the Presentation of the People Act 1983

---

[180] e.g.: Observer&Guardian v. the United Kingdom, judgment of 26.11.1991, ECHR.
This case was brought to the Court by The Observer, a publisher of the United Kingdom national Sunday newspaper. The Observer and the Guardian published short articles of the Spycatcher (the memoirs of one of the former employees of the MI5) which dealt with the unconstitutional and criminal conducting of some of the MI5 (British Security Service) officers. Many of the released information has already been published elsewhere. A permanent injunction, by the reason of breach of confidence, was achieved by the Attorney General. A few newspapers published the material of the Spycatcher; in conclusion, the judges of the Independent case basically announced that the injunction was necessary to preserve the confidentiality, hence, if further material would be released an inference with the administration of justice would likely be the result. Mr Wright, who wrote the Spycatcher, was responsible for not disclosing such information, hence, by neglecting this duty, he breached his obligations. The question was, whether or not a breach of Article 10 was given. This was affirmed by the Court. Moreover, it needed to be clarified if the interlocutory injunction was necessary in order to fulfill the social needs and if such a limitation of free speech targeted legitimate and proportionate aims. To sum up, the Court held that there was a violation of Article 10 in the period from 1987 to 1988 on the grounds of a lacking necessity in a democratic society because newspapers were prevented from the exercise of their right to purvey information.

[181] Hirst v. the United Kingdom, judgment of 06.10.2005, para. 3 to 4, ECHR.

he was excluded from parliamentary or local elections. Hence, he filed a complaint which states that violations of Article 3 of Protocol No. 1, Article 3 of Protocol 1 in conjunction with Article 14 because of discrimination and Article 10 based on the argumentation that the right to vote is a common form of expression.[182]

β) The argumentation regarding a violation of Article 3 ECHR

Regarding the first alleged violation the Court argued as follows 'The Court will therefore determine whether the measure in question pursued a legitimate aim in a proportionate manner having regard to the principles identified[...]. The Court points out that Article 3 of Protocol No. 1 does not, like other provisions of the Convention, specify or limit the aims which a restriction must pursue. A wide range of purposes may therefore be compatible with Article 3[...]the measure pursues the aim of preventing crime by sanctioning the conduct of convicted prisoners and also of enhancing civic responsibility and respect for the rule of law. The Court notes that, at the time of the passage of the latest legislation, the Government stated that the aim of the bar on convicted prisoners was to confer an additional punishment.'[183] In addition to that the Court said: 'The Court notes that the Chamber found that the measure lacked proportionality, essentially as it was an automatic blanket ban imposed on all convicted prisoners which was arbitrary in its effects and could no longer be said to serve the aim of punishing the applicant once his tariff (that period representing retribution and deterrence) had expired.'[184] In respect of the legitimate aims the Court held that they do not, per se, contravene the Conventions' ideology and, consequently, achieving an additional punishment in form of excluding from elections during the time in prison is justified. The Court announces that it cannot think of any circumstances which would possibly lead to an unsustainable or non-defendable result regarding the aim and the modernity of it. In respect of the proportionality of the act it noted that the system of restrictions of prisoners varies for divergent reasons, which according to the Court was less rough in comparison to other countries. Nonetheless, it criticized that 'It imposed a blanket restriction on all convicted prisoners. It applied automatically to all such prisoners, irrespective of the length of their sentence and irrespective of the nature or gravity of their offense. A prisoner sentenced to a week's imprisonment for a minor infraction might lose the right to vote if detained over election day, whereas a prisoner serving several years for a more serious crime might, by chance, avoid missing an election.'[185] Besides these arguments, the Court also noted that although no common sense is given within Europe the right to vote in the UK is revoked at the immediate moment of conviction which is not proportionate. The Government emphasized on the

[182] Hirst v. the United Kingdom, judgment of 06.10.2005, ECHR.
[183] Hirst v. the United Kingdom, judgment of 06.10.2005, para. 73 to 74, ECHR.
[184] Hirst v. the United Kingdom, judgment of 06.10.2005, para. 76, ECHR.
[185] Hirst v. the United Kingdom, judgement of 06.10.2005, para. 82, ECHR.

fact that, because of the lack of consensus, the range of approaches in order to exclude persons from voting has to be possible if the merit is serious that it results in imprisonment. The argumentation is based on the thought of the margin of appreciation but the Court assumed that a less narrow margin has to be the measure and that the UK could not solely rely on its tradition. The right to vote was seen as violated.[186]

γ) The significance of the dissenting opinions on the case

The case is of significance also because of the joint dissenting opinions which concluded that there has not been any violation of the right to vote and that the Court limits the responsibility of the State too drastically. Judges Wildhaber, Costa, Lorenzen, Kovler and Jebens stated that 'As Article 3 ECHR of Protocol No. 1 does not prescribe what aims may justify restrictions of the protected rights, such restrictions cannot in our opinion be limited to the lists set out in the second paragraphs of Articles 8 ECHR to 11 ECHR. Furthermore, we would point out that the Convention institutions in their case-law have to date been very careful not to challenge the aims relied on by the respondent Government to justify the restriction of a right under the Convention or its Protocols.'[187] The judges laid focus on the argument that a utilization of a wide narrow of margin of appreciation needs to be preserved.

Consequently the judges said that: 'the margin of appreciation in this area is wide, and have rightly paid attention to the numerous ways of organizing and running electoral systems and the wealth of differences in this field in terms of, inter alia, historical development, cultural diversity and political thought within Europe. Nonetheless, the majority have concluded that a general restriction on voting for persons serving a prison sentence 'must be seen as falling outside any acceptable margin of appreciation, however wide that margin might be'.'[188] They questioned if the majority considered the aspect of a 'dynamic and evolutive' interpretation in a realistic sense. 'As the majority have considered that it is not the role of the Court to indicate what, if any, restrictions on the right of serving prisoners to vote would be compatible with the Convention[...] implies that all States with such restrictions will face difficult assessments as to whether their legislation complies with the requirements of the Convention.'[189]

δ) Conclusion

The conclusion according to them is that there is no common ground within Europe because the regulations are far too divergent by the time of the decision. They also concluded that the Court is

---

[186] e.g.: Hirst v. the United Kingdom, judgement of 06.10.2005, ECHR.
[187] Hirst v. the United Kingdom, judgement of 06.10.2005, para. 3, ECHR.
[188] Hirst v. the United Kingdom, judgment of 06.10.2005, para. 5, ECHR.
[189] Hirst v. the United Kingdom, judgment of 06.10.2005, para 6, ECHR.

not a legislative organ firstly; secondly, that the concerned terms have to be carefully considered because of their unclarity which the Court oversaw. The dissenting opinions also imply that it is merely an assumption that the UK did not consider their legislation and that it is disharmony within European comparison. They claimed that there is no argument which is convincing enough to find the approach arbitrary or even cut off the right of expression. 'The point is that one must avoid confusing the ideal to be attained and which I support – which is to make every effort to bring the isolation of convicted prisoners to an end, even when they have been convicted of the most serious crimes, and to prepare for their reintegration into society and citizenship – and the reality of Hirst (no. 2), which on the one hand theoretically asserts a wide margin of appreciation for the States as to the conditions in which a subjective right (derived from judicial interpretation!) may be exercised, but goes on to hold that there has been a violation of that right, thereby depriving the State of all margin and all means of appreciation.'[190] Judge Costa claimed that it is absurd to guarantee a wide margin when reducing it if the question of proportionality arises. He insists on the point that the exceptions delivered within qualified rights are not exhaustive because the Court, paradoxically, did not consider to make exceptions in accordance of a general rule or defining them in a broader sense.[191]

ff. Criticism on the margin of appreciation through the Hatton-case

The instrument of the margin of appreciation not only achieved positive critiques but also serious criticism based on several arguments which will be illustrated. Further criticism on the margin of appreciation was revealed in the Hatton-case, but also in the Buckley-case where the margin of appreciation construed as such, that the Court drew the conclusion of no violated provisions.[192]

---

[190] Hirst v. the United Kingdom, judgement of 06.10.2005, para. 9, ECHR.
[191] Hirst v. the United Kingdom, judgment of 06.10.2005, ECHR.
[192] Hatton and others v. the United Kingdom, judgement of 08.07.2003, ECHR.
Buckley v. the United Kingdom, judgment of 25.09.1996, ECHR.
This case was referred to the Court by the Commission as well as by the Government of Northern Ireland and the United Kingdom of Great Britain. The applicant lived with her three children in caravans which were placed in land owned by herself. The land of the applicant was part of a group which were all Gypsies. Some of them received a permanent planning permission in order to be able to use the caravans residential. The complainant was refused for a planning permission on the grounds that the planned usage of her land would detract from the open landscape, further, that the accommodation for Gypsies reached its point of saturation and that the local development would be in danger. The Court had to vet if the applicant was violated in Article 8 taken together with Article 14 of the Convention on the grounds of preventing her from pursuing a traditional lifestyle and being criminalized of unauthorized camping. By the fact that Gypsies considered lifestyle as living in caravans and traveling, the Court stated that the applicant's private life was concerned as well. Therefore, her property had to be classified as her home. Consequently, the ECtHR questioned whether or not her right to respect her home suffered from interferences. On the ground that she was forced to remove her caravan by the authorities and, further, prosecuted for failing to do so, the applicant undoubtedly underwent an interference. Without proper examination, the Court found that the interference was in accordance with the law and that the Government pursued legitimate aims and measures to enforce the aims. Still, the ECtHR analyzed properly if the interference was necessary for the society. That was when the Court examined the scope of the margin of appreciation and concluded that a wide margin of appreciation seemed to be legitimate. The ECtHR, therefore, laid focus on the fact that it did not want to replace the

Consequently it is necessary to analyze the cases mentioned above, in order to understand the consequences and the impact of this principle.

(1) The case of Hatton v. the UK

α) The facts

This case dealt with a possible interference of Article 8 ECHR. As to the facts, summarized it can be said that the applicants complained about a newly introduced scheme regarding the regulation of night-transfer of aircrafts. This scheme allowed aircraft operators to choose a greater amount of quiet aircrafts so that the statutory boundary of acoustic level would not have been overstepped. This regulation would be unlawfully in respect of the Civil Aviation Act 1982.[193]

β) The argumentation of the ECtHR regarding a violation of Article 8 ECHR

The Court held that there has been a violation of Article 8 ECHR as to the following main reasons, 'The Court has no doubt that the implementation of the 1993 Scheme was susceptible of adversely affecting the quality of the applicants' private life and the scope for their enjoying the amenities of their respective homes, and thus their rights protected by Article 8 of the Convention. Each of the applicants had described the way in which he or she was affected by the changes brought about by the 1993 Scheme at the relevant time'[194]. Although the disadvantages were not directly caused by the State, it has an obligation and responsibility to regulate the private industry sector so that the fundamental rights are well protected. In addition to that, it declared that a proper investigation has to be made in order to conclude if the economic interests were struck in a fair balance to the interests of the applicants. It considered that 'Whether in the implementation of that regime the right balance has been struck in substance between the Article 8 ECHR rights affected by the regime and other conflicting community interests depends on the relative weight given to each of them. The Court accepts that in this context the authorities were entitled, having regard to the general nature of the measures taken, to rely on statistical data[...].'[195] Because of the importance of the London airport one easily could understand the need for maintenance of a full service. Although, studies have revealed information that indicate that particular night flights could be eliminated; the Court found no grave link between night flights and regular flights. Obviously, the margin of appreciation was utilized, this led to the conclusion that the authorities did fulfilled the

---

national authorities actions or legislations but evaluating the local conditions and needs of the democratic society. It weighed the interests of the applicant and those of the authorities. In conclusion, the Court found that there was no breach of Article 8 of the Convention based on the arguments that reasons the authorities relied on were sufficient and relevant on order to justify the interference.

[193] Hatton and others v. the United Kingdom, judgment of 08.07.2003, ECHR.

[194] Hatton and others v. the United Kingdom, judgment of 08.07.2003, para. 118, ECHR.

[195] Hatton and others v. the United Kingdom, judgment of 08.07.2003, para. 125, ECHR.

required measures so to be justified within the infringement and consequently no violation of Article 8 ECHR was recognized.[196] The question is 'How could an economic interest interfere in such a manner with a substantial right as the right of health'?

γ) Conclusion and critical remarks

An aftertaste remains concerning the aspect that an utilization of such a narrow margin of appreciation can be justified by the Court when weighting two interests. Further, one could impute base motives to the Courts' decision; did it not know about the circumstance that, if handing over the responsibility in the precarious matter to the contracting State, it would not come into an unpleasant situation? An unpleasant situation may have resulted from, e.g. the fact that it probably would have had to deal with further complaints of such difficult kind and assuming that the Court would have utilized a narrow margin, it obviously would have taken an unequivocal stand on the range of the right of health and environmental protection. If denying provisions such as a sufficient health protection in comparison to economic interests and conducts, one could question if the Court provides sufficient protection but only up to a particular point. And namely this point would be the risk of challenging troublesome dialogues with the Member States because economic interests are of significant importance to each national well-being. Besides that, the Court does not, as it did in a variety of decisions before, emphasize on the evolutive character of societal needs. It seems to be quite difficult to figure out the reasons behind its decision; because of the artificial character of the reasoning. Did the Court solely wanted to 'keep its hands clean' regarding the highly precarious territory of economic?[197]

δ) Dissenting opinions

Although the opinion of the ECtHR is most cited and carried over by other courts, this does not imply that this happens to be 'the one right opinion'. Therefore the joint dissenting opinions of the former case shall reveal divergent chain of thoughts. The joint dissenting opinions of the judges Costa, Ress, Türmen, Zupančič and Steiner include but are not limited to these thoughts. They referred to the European Unions' Charter of Fundamental Rights concerning the environmental protection was one of the highest goods to improve 'These recommendations show clearly that the Member States of the European Union want a high level of protection and better protection, and expect the Union to develop policies aimed at those objectives.[...]the question of environmental pollution is a supra-national one, as it knows no respect for the boundaries of national sovereign-

[196] Hatton and others v. the United Kingdom, judgment of 08.07.2003, ECHR.
[197] e.g.: Hatton and others v. the United Kingdom, judgment of 08.07.2003, para. 118, ECHR.

ty'[198]. In addition to that, the dissenting opinion captured another highly relevant principle when arguing 'This 'evolutive' interpretation by the Commission and the Court of various Convention requirements has generally been 'progressive', in the sense that they have gradually extended and raised the level of protection afforded to the rights and freedoms guaranteed by the Convention to develop the 'European public order'. In the field of environmental human rights, which was practically unknown in 1950, the Commission and the Court have increasingly taken the view that Article 8 embraces the right to a healthy environment; hence, the protection against pollution and nuisances caused by harmful chemicals, offensive smells, agents which precipitate respiratory ailments, noise and so on.'[199] They also pointed out that it is absurd to ignore the main problem in the case when similar applications were declared admissible before. Of course, this does not immediately conclude that a violation is given but obviously points out that there is an unsolved issue. Of great significance is the following passage, 'The majority tries to distinguish the present case from Dudgeon v. the United Kingdom [...], which dealt with the sexual intimacy aspect of the applicant's private life. In Dudgeon [...] 'The present case concerns a most intimate aspect of private life. Accordingly, there must exist particularly serious reasons before interferences on the part of the public authorities can be legitimate for the purposes of paragraph 2 of Article 8.' The majority judgment differentiates this case from Dudgeon by saying: 'the sleep disturbances relied on by the applicants did not intrude into an aspect of private life in a manner comparable to that of the criminal measures considered in Dudgeon to call for an especially narrow scope for the State's margin of appreciation.'[200] The aspect of privacy is of great societal interest because drastic interference can cost physical or psychological illness. The physical and mental well-being definitely overlaps with the protection of health. Besides, the judges question the argumentation behind the term 'discomfort' of the passengers which could affect the functioning of the airport and would interfere with the economic interests. Does the discomfort of a minority disclose them because the majority needs to be protected from discomfort or is it the main achievement of human rights to safeguard the minority in specific? Finally, they stated that 'Incidentally, the Court's own subsidiary role, reflected in the use of the 'margin of appreciation', is itself becoming even more and more marginal when it comes to such situations as the relationship between the protection of the right to sleep as an aspect of privacy and health on the one hand and the very general economic interest on the other hand.'[201]

[198] Hatton and others v. the United Kingdom, judgment of 08.07.2003, para. 1, ECHR.
[199] Hatton and others v. the United Kingdom, judgment of 08.07.2003, para. 2, ECHR.
[200] Hatton and others v. the United Kingdom, judgment of 08.07.2003, para.9, ECHR
Dudgeon v. the United Kingdom, judgment of 22.10.1981, ECHR.
[201] Hatton v. the United Kingdom, judgment of 08.07.2003, para. 17, ECHR.

2. Excursus: An insight to further ECtHR related interpretation mechanisms

The principles illustrated above are of great importance but of course not the only mechanisms which were generated by the European Court of Human Rights. To offer a complete insight to the work of the Court, a few further important methods of interpretation and principles will be discussed at this juncture; hence a conjunction between the single arguments of the Court can be made more easily.

a. The autonomous interpretation

The ECHR uses undefined demotic terms such as private, liberty, family, work;or phrases used within the field of technique or science like judge, lawful detention, independent, etc. The question is in what sense these 'termini' have to be defined. The ECtHR independently defines specific terms without having consideration for the particular States definition within their national system. Article 31 states that everyday language expressions have to be defined within an ordinary meaning given by the Court. Regarding scientific terms the Court avoids any controversies but adapts the meanings given by acknowledged specialists if it can be justified and does not suffer from a lack of reasonability. Slightly more difficulties emerge if it comes to legal 'termini'. The boundary has to be laid down whether the States' definition or the Courts' meaning can be taken. By this time the Court follows the path to apply autonomous meanings. An autonomous interpretation is much more complex than it appears at the first look. E.g. the Engel-case[202] in respect of Article 6 ECHR which states 'In the determination of his civil rights and obligations or of any criminal charge against him, everyone is entitled to a fair and public hearing within a reasonable time by an independent and impartial tribunal established by law.'[203] The claimant accused the military courts of violating Article 6 ECHR by imposing sanctions in case of military offences based on the fact that the requirements of proceedings executed by the authorities are not sufficient. On the other hand it was argued that 'For both the Government and the Commission, the proceedings brought against [...] involved the determination neither of 'civil rights and obligations' nor of 'any criminal charge'.'[204] Furthermore, it stated that Article 6 ECHR is not applicable under the given circumstances because the imposition of military sanctions has not been investigated under criminal rules. Military penalties are of a disciplinary nature only. Interestingly, the Court argued as following 'It must thus be asked whether or not the solution adopted in this connection at the national level is decisive from the standpoint of the Convention. Does Article 6 [...] cease to be applicable just because the competent organs of a Contracting State classify as disciplinary an act or omission and the proceedings it takes against the author, or does it, on the contrary, apply in certain cases notwithstanding

---

202 Engel and others v. the Netherlands, judgment of 08.06.1976, ECHR.
203 in Appendix.
204 Engel and others v. the Netherlands, judgment of 08.06.1976, para. 79, ECHR.

this classification? [...] The Court has devoted attention to the respective submissions of the applicants, the Government and the Commission concerning what they termed the 'autonomy' of the concept of a 'criminal charge', but does not entirely subscribe to any of these submissions.'[205] According to the Court this distinction can be well reflected and due to a particular practice not unjustified. Besides, States while following the public interest are free within their performance of making such distinctions. But regarding the nature of the two options of handling, the disciplinary punishment is much less severe in comparison to a criminal litigation and it has to be seen in the light of the Convention. Since then, the ECtHR developed particular methods to correctly apply the autonomous mechanism on the one hand and respecting the by national authorities within their legal system defined termini on the other. The determination of the Member State has relative value only which means further analysis is needed to follow; otherwise, if not sufficiently and wide-spread considered, autonomous handling would possibly lead to a kind of 'being an active legislator'.[206]

b. The comparative interpretation

The Purpose of the Convention always needs to be considered firstly. If it comes to undefined terms the institution organs not only need to develop autonomous definitions to cope with the ECHR and its objectives. The so called comparative interpretation is a mechanism which refers to defined or worked out definitions complemented in other international treaties, agreements or legal acts. The Court did so e.g. in the Marckx-case [207], where the issue had to be decided on as to whether Belgian family law regarding the situation of illegitimate children was compatible with the Convention. The matter concerned the particular question whether the domestic Belgium law, which is compatible with one international legal act could possibly contravene to an other agreement which was compiled and signed by the same parties? The Court held that '[...] In this case, the Court cannot but be struck by the fact, that the domestic law of the great majority of the Member States of the Council of Europe has evolved and is continuing to evolve, in company with the relevant international instruments, towards full juridical recognition of the maxim 'mater semper certa est'.[208] Admittedly, of the ten States that drew up the Brussels Convention, only eight have signed and only four have ratified it to date. The European Convention of 15 October 1975 on the Legal Status of Children born out of Wedlock has at present been signed by only ten and ratified by only four Members of the Council of Europe.[...] Both the relevant Conventions are in force and there is no reason to attribute the currently small number of Contracting States to a refusal to admit equality between

---

205 Engel and others v. the Netherlands, judgment of 08.06.1976, para. 80 to 81, ECHR.

206 e.g.: Macdonald R.St.J., Matscher F., Petzold H., *The European System for the Protection of Human Rights*. (1993).

207 Marckx v. Belgium, judgment of 13.06.1979, ECHR.

208 e.g.: Macdonald R.St.J., Matscher F., Petzold H., *The European System for the Protection of Human Rights*. (1993).

'illegitimate' and 'legitimate' children on the point under consideration. In fact, the existence of these two treaties denotes that there is a clear measure of common ground in this area amongst modern societies.'[209]

c. Proportionality

The principle of proportionality is, besides the margin of appreciation, one of the most important techniques to examine the reasonableness of restrictions. The core can be reduced to one phrase namely 'necessity and appropriateness'. The Convention itself does not explicitly imply the idea of proportionality but if regarding the Convention intently and as a whole, several occasions arise where proportionality could be subsumed as inherent to it. For example, Article 15 states that derogation is justified in 'time of war or other public emergency threatening the life of the nation'. Besides, qualified rights do offer certain mediate proportionality, e.g. when stating that an act has to be in accordance with the 'necessity in a democratic society'. 'From 'necessity' to proportionality is but a small step, since for a measure to be necessary it must surely correspond to a 'pressing social need' both as a matter of principle[...]'.[210]

aa. The four question test generated by the ECtHR

The case-law offers quite an adequate definition and on basis of that definition the Court formulated a 'four question test', 'The principle of proportionality requires that there be a reasonable relationship between particular objective to be achieved and the means used to achieve that objective.[...]

· Is there a pressing social need for some restriction of the Convention?
· If so, does the particular restriction correspond to this need?
· If so, is it a proportionate response to that need?
· In any case, are the reasons presented by the authorities, relevant and sufficient?'[211]

bb. Criticism towards the principle of Proportionality

But also criticism arose whether or not the principle of proportionality is a valid method because it merely weights morals against each other based on precast opinions and does not have a deeper look into the origin of them. This may lead to the consequence that the real moral matter remains unsolved and it only contains an artificial solution. The Court is forced to take account of several factors when drawing a conclusion in respect of whether or not an interference is proportionate. If no justification is assumed the fundamental provision would be impaired and as a consequence inappropriate. The principle obviously bounces between the margin of appreciation of the States

209 Marckx v. Belgium, judgment of 13.06.1979, para. 40 to 41, ECHR.
210 Eissen M. in *The European System for the Protection of Human Rights* (1993), p.126.
211 http://www.coe.int/t/dghl/cooperation/lisbonnetwork/themis/echr/paper2_en.asp, retrieved 31.08.2013. also utilized in Handyside v. the United Kingdom, judgment of 07.12.1976, ECHR.

and the Courts' supervisory role which logically leads to the consequence that it divers from case to case whether or not the reasoning reaches up to be proportionate. In addition to that, it depends on the case to what extent the proportionality is examined which solely lies within the competence of the Court.[212]

C. Conclusive remarks

Jean-Claude Mignon, president of the Parliamentary Assembly of the Council of Europe, said 'But the real problem [...] is that the court was never supposed to be a substitute for national protection of human rights. It was always meant to play a subsidiary or "back up" role. [...]setting the standard for human rights protection not just in Europe but across the world. It has been a catalyst for positive change in many new democracies, contributing to long-term "deep security" across the whole continent, while occasionally nudging even advanced democracies in the right direction. Its civilising influence is deeply precious. Let's fix it while we still can.'[213] When getting to the bottom of the difficulties, which the ECtHR is confronted with, Mignon is absolutely right regarding the fact that the ECtHR was assigned to be in a supplementary position, but in fact, the Court has a completely different and subtle role by now, and the judgments of the Court seem to resume some legislative functions of the Member States. As we have seen above, the Court explored and developed methods in order to cope with the requirements of its position/work, but are these methods adequate and is the way of the utilization of them in compliance with equality, human rights and fundamental freedoms? When having a closer look at the utilization of the methods of interpretation, it clearly can be observed that the Court balances the diverse interests in different ways, depending on the case and the parties concerned, which leads to the questions 'Where is a boundary, so that the divergent interpretation cannot be defined as arbitrariness?', 'Does the ECtHR try to avoid delicate situations, when it comes to politically influenced cases, where some invisible powerful actors may be the protagonists but not the Court?' or 'Is it simply ineffective and too early to be definite in an unreflected manner regarding specific issues, because of the circumstance that the Court has to include such a broad spectrum of individuals?'

The principles seem to be an efficient measure to utilize adapted parameters, but still the manner of utilization has to be deliberated in order to guarantee an objective 'evidence' for each decision, which some cases were definitely lacking of and no stringent argumentation was observable. Further, the development of the work of the ECtHR and its methods, especially when the margin of appreciation is utilized, is not yet predictable in detail, due to the fast changing morals, needs,

---

[212] e.g.: Tsakyrakis Stavros, *Proportionality: An Assault on Human Rights?,* Jean Monnet Working Paper 09/08, 2012, http://centers.law.nyu.edu/jeanmonnet/papers/08/080901.pdf, retrieved 31.08.2013.

[213] http://www.theguardian.com/law/2012/apr/19/european-court-of-human-rights-human-rights, retrieved 03.12.2013.

definitions, lifestyles, problems, etc within the European society. On the other hand, the States obviously do need to accept that the protection of human rights is of essential necessity, and therefore, it is unavoidable to establish national legal basis for such protection. To sum up: The Court still is the last instance for individuals in order to combat human rights violations.

Section Four:

I. The legal machinery

A. The substantive power of the legal machinery regarding the Admissibility

1. The impact of implementing Protocol No. 11

Since Protocol No. 11 entered into force on the 1.11.1998, the decision of admissibility became the province of the ECtHR as complaints are referred directly to it. Inter-State cases can be brought up by any High-Court of a Member State according to Article 33 of the renewed Convention. Regarding complaints from individuals Article 34 newly offers a direct application to the Court. Nevertheless a Committee of the Court is in charge of striking out applications, deciding with final consequence, if it appears to be possible without any thorough examination. Article 37 enumerates certain criteria to strike out an application at any stage of the proceedings, as these are the case that an applicant does not intend to pursue his application, the case of an already resolved matter or if it comes to the situation that any reasons are given which no longer justify the continuation of a further examination. If a decision has not been rendered which could be an outcome of a dissent on an opinion pro inadmissibility or a decision is either favored, then a Chamber composed of seven judges attends to the case. [214]

2. The admissibility criteria

Article 35 manifests the three criteria of admissibility; it says that 'The Court may only deal with the matter after all domestic remedies have been exhausted, according to generally recognized rules of international law, and within a period of six months from the date on which the final decision was taken.'[215]

a. The criteria of exhaustion of all remedies

The criteria of exhausting all national remedies, which is the focus, is examined within the famous case of Earl Spencer, where the court declared the case inadmissible.[216] Because of the importance of this specific criteria the case mentioned above will illustrate the meaning, impact and consequences of such a criteria by a short description.

aa. The case of Earl Spencer v. the United Kingdom

Several newspapers published private information about the deteriorated health condition of Countess Spencer who at that time found herself at a clinic specialized on eating disorders. Further information and details had been press released about the marriage of the Spencer's and certain

---

[214] in Appendix.
[215] in Appendix.
[216] Earl and Countess Spencer v. United Kingdom, judgment of 16.01.1998, ECHR.

affairs. The applicant complained at the Press Complaints Committee alleging a violation of their private life. The PCC is a non-statutory body, which is in charge of regulating conflicts regarding press releases. In the concerned case the issue came up whether all domestic remedies were exhausted because there is no law protecting the privacy in England but the Statutes of the PCC which manifests that a breach of confidence in the sense of a remedy is given, if the necessity of confidence is given within the information itself, the information must have been used without authorization and the circumstances under which the information was published demand an obligation of confidence.[217] The question is if the national authorities violated an obligation to protect private life and did not offer an effective domestic remedy?[218]

The Commission noted that an effective remedy may also involve the adoption of effective devices.'[...]to exhaust remedies which relate to the breaches[...]. Accordingly the Government must establish that the remedy in question was accessible, was one capable of providing redress in respect of the applicant's complaint and offered reasonable prospects of success.'[219] The Commission declared that a conclusion implying that a remedy is ineffective by verifying a breach of confidence is not sufficient but a national Court should have the possibility attending the specific matter in order to underline given rights through establishing ways to interpret them. Furthermore, the Court has to declare inadmissibility in cases of anonymous applications or matters which already have been examined by the Court or became a matter of other international investigation procedures as well as settlements and do not contain new relevant facts understood as information.[220]

bb. The case of X v. Iceland

The Court also strikes out applications if the concerned issue is incompatible with the ECHR and its protocols or simply aims an abusive usage of fundamental rights or ill-founded as so decided in the Iceland case.[221] The commission had to deal with the electoral system in Iceland which so the claimant contravenes with Article 3 of Protocol No. 1 in respect of assuring the individual right to vote provided by elections, because of not considering the matter of equality within the vote. In fact Article 3 does not offer an individual right to one man- one vote because the provision of the equality of the vote is not implied within the concerned right. '[...]free expression of the opinion of the people primarily signify that the elections cannot under any form of pressure in the choice of one or more candidates[...]'.[222] Obviously the Court tried to obey being part of political saying

[217] Janis M.W., Kay R.S., Bradley A.W., *European human Rights Law (2008), p.33.*
[218] Earl and Countess Spencer v. United Kingdom, judgment of 16.01.1998, ECHR.
[219] Janis M.W., Kay R.S., Bradley A.W., *European human Rights Law (2008), p. 34.*
[220] Earl and Countess Spencer v. United Kingdom, judgment of 16.01.1998, ECHR.
[221] e.g.: Janis M.W., Kay R.S., Bradley A.W., *European human Rights Law (2008), p. 87.*
[222] X v. Iceland, judgment of 08.12.1981, ECHR.

within the Member States. Without any further investigation it declared the case as ill-founded. On a deeper look this seemed to be logical and understandable regarding the fact that if it would have dealt with the merits it probably would have had e.g. further complaints. If so, did the Court want to decide in cases where electoral systems of States of more political and economical power as the U.K., France, Germany, etc. were subjected to an investigation? In respect of the reasons,principles and political motivations as well as controlling and sanction mechanisms of the ECHR nowadays the question seems self-answering. Regarding the origin of the establishment of the ECHR the question arises where do the organs have to trespass the 'boundaries' of States and by virtue of crossing this ostensible unbreakable line recognize e.g. totalitarian political systems?[223]

3 . Excursus: The scope of an application respectively acting exterritorial

In 2001 the Court itself decided on a famous case; the Bankovich-case;[224] Regarding the cited criteria above, the application of criterions was discussed. Bankovich claimed violations of Articles 2, 10 and 13 ECHR. The case did not only prompt questions in the light of legal aspects but also regarding political interests and explicitly the question of the extent of fundamental human rights regarding the obligations of the contracting States. The claimants were victims of a missile which bombed a target and killed or/and injured certain people. The applicant argued that there is no further protection of their rights rather than that of the ECHR and that the actors did not only need to respect the obligations within their territory but also when acting exterritorial. While exercising air sovereignty over Yugoslavia they would have had to appreciate the fundamental rights. The argumentation of the defendants is congruent with the courts final decision in terms of the question whether the bombardment brought the plaintiffs under the concerned jurisdictions. 'The Governments dispute the admissibility of the case. They mainly contend that the application is incompatible ratione personae with the provisions of the Convention because the applicants did not fall within the jurisdiction of the respondent States within the meaning of Article 1 of the Convention.'[225] Furthermore the Court expounded that the ECHR has to be interpreted in the light of the Vienna Convention 1969. '[...] must also take in account any relevant rules of international law when examining questions concerning its jurisdiction and, consequently, determine State responsibility in conformity with the governing principles of international law, although it must remain mindful of the Convention's character as a human rights treaty[...].'[226] Therefore, the Court, further on noted that it concerns a territorial notion of the ECHR which led to the fact that only under exceptional

[223] e.g.: X v. Iceland, judgment of 08.12.1981, ECHR.
[224] Bankovic and others v. Belgium, the Czech Republic, Denmark, France, Germany, Greece, Hungary, Iceland, Italy, Luxembourg, the Netherlands, Norway, Poland, Portugal, Spain, Turkey and the United Kingdom, judgment of 12.12.2001, ECHR.
[225] Bankovic et al. v. Belgium, judgment of 12.12.2001, 31, ECHR.
[226] Bankovic et al. v. Belgium, judgment of 12.12.2001, 57.

circumstances any actions by contracting States outside the territory do constitute the performance of jurisdiction in the light of Article 1 ECHR because it was not the intention to expand the rights in such a manner. The Court also argued with similar mannered cases.[227] Consequently the argumentation led to the conclusion of inadmissibility under the aspect of incompatibility with the Convention. The question remains whether fundamental rights should be far more reaching than expected and if so, did the Court handle this obstacles with consistency or not and for what possibly sustainable reasons happened the decision to be entirely different in the Loizidou-case [228]?

In fact, this case brought up many questions which mostly are of academic nature to solve e.g. in the Case of Smith v. Secretary of State of Defense [229], where the question arose if a military servant

---

[227] e.g.: Spencer J.R., *Extradition, the European Arrest Warrant and Human Rights,* The Cambridge Law Journal, Volume 72, July 2013, pp. 250-253.
Soering v. the United Kingdom, judgment of 07.07.1989, ECHR.
The applicant in the following case was a born as a German national and brought to the United States at the age of eleven. He was imprisoned in England and was waiting for the extradition to the United States of America to face charges of murdering two people in Virginia. The United States of America requested the extradition of the two of them according to the Extradition Treaty 1972 between the States concerned. The United Kingdom sought an assurance on the matter of the death penalty, further, if it would come to such events, Mr. Soering would not be subject of a carried out death penalty. A further application by Soering in order to gain a judicial review was refused. Moreover, he stated that he probably would be sentenced to death, although an prohibiting assurance existed; further, that there was a severe likelihood that he would be a victim of the 'death row phenomenon' which would thereby lead to an inhuman and degrading treatment causing a breach of Article 3 ECHR. The Commission reaffirmed that there is the possibility that individuals will be subjected to degrading treatment in case of an extradition or deportation. Regarding the fact that the United States are not addressees of the Convention, the Convention embodies the obligation not to subject a person to a degrading punishment set by an other State. The Court concluded that Article 1 provides territorial boundaries to the applicable rights and freedoms. The Convention has to be interpreted and applied so as to make its safeguards effective. By the reason of the real and substantial risks of exposure, the ECtHR held that there exists an inherent obligation to extend the territorial impact of the Convention's rights. Summarized it is to be said that the Court found a breach of Article 3 because the death row phenomenon has to be classified as exceptional and intense situation which is degrading as well as inhuman.

[228] Loizidou v. Turkey, judgment of 18.12.1996, ECHR.

[229] Smith v. Secretary of State for Defence, http://www.equalityhumanrights.com/legal-and-policy/legal-updates/the-smith-case/, retrieved 31.08.2013.
The case dealt with a complaint against the authorities in charge because of the fact that a Private suffered a cardiac arrest and was pronounced dead by the reason of hyperthermia. Before that event, he called in sick and complained about his medical constitution. The family of the Private filed a complaint on the grounds of preventing them to have an insight to the crucial documents, further on, they noted that sufficient medical appliance has not been provided. The High Court decided that the Human Rights Act needed to be applied to all armed forces who are serving, no matter whether or not their death took place on a base of the army. Logically this meant that the life of the soldiers needed to be protected properly and adequate facilities/supplies had to be offered. The Court of Appeal, the Supreme Court, overturned the High Court's decision and findings. Additionally, it found that it is the obligation of the ECtHR to decide whether or not the law should be extended in order to cover military personnel in case of leaving the base.
e.g.: Loizidou v. Turkey, judgment of 18.12.1996, ECHR.
This case was referred to the Court by the Government of the Republic of Cypress. The applicant was a Cypriot national who stated that she has been prevented in the past, and is still prevented, from enjoying her property. She attended in a march in order to assert the right of Greek Cypriot refugees to return back home. She got arrested and the detention has been kept on. Several declarations have been made and renewed by Turkey and Cypress as well; mainly dealing with the jurisdiction ratione materiae in respect of Article 25. On the grounds of the detention the applicant claimed violations of Articles 3,5 and 8 of the ECHR. Further on, she complained that refusing her to access her property constituted a continuing violation of Article 1 of Protocol No. 1. The ECtHR considered that the Government of Turkey referred the case by the reason of questioning the competence, further, such a motivation did not seem to be inherent to an abuse of its procedures. Although the political situations were difficult, the Court held that Turkey was the respondent

falls under the jurisdiction if not being linked to the UK territory. Again, it has been argued that it is not the essence of the ECHR to expand the jurisdiction but only in cases of exceptions which are still not explicitly defined yet. Although recognizing a link between humanitarian law, international law and military actions, the majority of the Supreme Court did find it negotiable establishing jurisdiction within military actions under such circumstances but nevertheless it affirmatively referred to the argumentation of the Al-Skeini case [230], in which the UK was found guilty of violating the ECHR caused by the denial of investigation of killings of Iraqi civilians by British soldiers during an invasion in Iraq. The ECtHR referenced the interpretation of law of the ICJ in order to specify the discrepancies between international humanitarian law and human rights law. The ICJ clearly formulated that while exercising exterritorial, human rights law could be applied; especially in cases of occupation of other territories.[231] The ECtHR argued that an extension could be granted if there is a given authority in form of controlling other individuals. Still such exceptions should be limited and actually being applied if it can be spoken of physical controlling or commanding of others. Conclusively the matter remains unanswered and new questions arose, for example, where is difference between denying responsibility and authority in case of killings by missiles and on the opposite in case of having public power over individuals regarding the right to life?

B. Controlling mechanism

1. Inter- State applications

Article 33 ECHR regulates that 'Any High Contracting Party may refer to the Court any alleged breach of the provisions of the Convention and the protocols thereto by another High Contracting Party.'[232]

This means that none of the involved States do need to be considered as a victim because any State is able to lodge complaints concerning human rights violations or abuses committed against individuals by a contracting party. By the fact that the claimant does not need to characterize itself through being a victim, the cited Article gives a widespread competence ratione personae. In particular individuals further on do not need to be citizens of one of the Member States but if so,

party in this case, however, it admitted that the relevant principles of international law needed to be referenced. This impact found its source in the fact that turkish officials were involved, but Turkey did not happen to have accountable physical control over the territory concerned. To sum up, the Commission found that Turkey was responsible for the armed forces and consequently, responsible for the prevention of gaining access to the applicant's property. The Court followed that point of view and considered the issue capable to fall within the Turkish jurisdiction. By the reasons of the declaration of Turkey regarding the jurisdiction, the Court decided not to judge at the present phase of the ongoing procedure , it therefore, jointed the objection to the merits of the case.

230 Al-Skeini and others v. The United Kingdom, judgment of 07.07.2011, ECHR.

231 e.g.: Reports of Judgments of the International Court of Justice in the Case of Democratic Republic of the Congo v. Uganda, 19.12.2005, ICJ.

232 in Appendix.

this fact is no obstacle for a complaint. 'In this way the right of Inter-State complaint resembles an actio popularis.' [...] where a state complains about the legislation or administrative practices of another Contracting Party, the complaining state need not even assert that there are specific victims of the alleged violations.[233] In Ireland v. the United Kingdom the Court dealt with such a matter for the first time and in 2001 it repeated its point of view that administrative practices of states can cause an accusation 'by reason of an alleged administrative practice, including an alleged practice of failing to secure enjoyment of their possessions in southern Cyprus to Turkish Cypriots living in northern Cyprus.' [234]

2. Applications by individuals

The possibility to claim a violation by individuals is enshrined in Article 34 ECHR which says that 'The Court may receive applications from any person, non-governmental organization or group of individuals claiming to be the victim of a violation by one of the High Contracting Parties of the right set forth in the Convention or the protocols thereto. The High Contracting Parties undertake not to hinder in any way the effective exercise of this right'.[235] Article 34 ECHR probably provides the most significant and effective human rights protection mechanism. If an individual, excluding groups as such, is affected by a human rights abuse it can bring in a claim if specific requirements are fulfilled. In contrary to the Inter-State application there is no actio popularis provided which thus leading to the effect that a claim where several individuals complain violations each person

---

[233] Gomien D., *Short guide to the European Convention on Human Rights,*(2005) ,p.166.
[234] Ireland v. the United Kingdom, judgment of 18.01.1978, ECHR.
From the beginnings of 1920 onwards, the Northern Ireland had a separate Government and its own Parliament. Nevertheless, the society itself remained split, consisting of two communities, and, therefore never gained to become a homogenous society. Caused by these facts several bloody and fearful riots took place. The Irish Republican Army as a quasi-military organization never recognized the existence of Northern Ireland as a part of Great Britain, nor did it accept any democratic order of the Republic. Campaigns and terrorism followed repeatedly. As a consequence, the IRA was declared as an illegal organization by the legal authorities. Organizations were founded as a counterpart to the IRA. The disturbances, riots, battles and worsened, further, they gained intensity as well as cruelty/brutality. Several years later, the Government decided to introduce internment and detention as extrajudicial measures. On the grounds of these legalized internments, some operations followed. In accordance with this Regulation, people were arrested and interrogated. Later, these Regulations were converted into interim custody orders in order to combat the violence which put the public in fear. To sum up, by the reason of the development stated above 5 techniques (well-standing, hooding, subjection to noise, deprivation of sleep, food and drink) were developed to interrogate suspects accused of setting terrorist acts. These interrogation techniques were adopted by the Government of Northern Ireland and Great Britain. The ECtHR thus had to decide whether those interrogation techniques were a practice of inhuman and degrading treatment in the sense of Article 2 of the Convention. The Court found that the techniques did not reach the particular intensity and brutality which is implied within the word torture, but they were inhuman and degrading within the meaning of Article 3 of the ECHR. The Court generally noted that torture needs to attach a specific stigma in order to deliberate inhuman treatment which consequently causes severe suffering.
e.g.: Cypress v. Turkey, judgment of 10.05.2001, ECHR.
In this case the Court dealt with the question whether or not the case fell into the jurisdiction of Turkey and, therefore caused its responsibilities. The ECtHR reiterated its argumentation of the Loizidou judgment. Therefore, it can be referred to the detailed pleadings of that judgment. Summarized, it is to be said that Turkey was found guilty of violating Article 3,5 and 8 in specific.
[235] in Appendix.

itself has to allege being a victim. Besides, it is guaranteed that States are exhorted to desist from hindering the process of a claim, which has to be understood in the following sense 'The Court has held that the essence of this provision is to ensure that applicants or potential applicants can communicate freely with the Court without being subjected to any form of pressure from the authorities to withdraw or modify their complaints'.[236]

The case of Aktivar reveals certain circumstances whereby an applicant was hindered accessing particular domestic remedies, where after the required remedies in order to file a complaint of a violation to the ECtHR could not have been exhausted. 'The Court recalls its finding that, while the Turkish Government had shown the existence of a scheme of remedies under Turkish law to deal with complaints arising out of the struggle against terrorism, the action for compensation before the administrative courts could not be considered an effective remedy in respect of the applicant's complaint'.[237]

[236] Gomien D., *Short guide to the European Convention on Human Rights (*2005), *p. 168.*

[237] Case of Aktivar and others v. Turkey, 16.09.1996, ECHR.

This case found its origin in an application lodged by several Turkish nationals who were victims of an attack caused by the Parti Karkarani Kurdistan (Kurdistan Workers' Party). According to the claimants, the soldiers set fire to their houses and the major was forced to evacuate the village's inhabitants immediately. The Government, on the other hand, asserted that the villagers left their homes voluntarily. The security forces set up by the Government searched the evacuated village without causing any damages. The Government claimed that the applicants were not legitimized to file a complaint by the reason that the remedy has not been exhausted. The Court recalled that, this plea had to be rejected and, further, that the general principles had to be taken into account concerning the exhaustion of remedies. The ECtHR noted that no detailed investigation were made whether or not the illicit behavior of the security forces had occurred. The events took place in areas where Turkey was subject to martial law. Moreover, the Court stated that the circumstances of such insecure situations which are jeopardizing the applicant's security and threatening in general need to be taken into consideration. In respect of the Government's argument that administrative Courts were in charge to deal with the complaint, the Court announced that a remedy before an administrative institution would not be efficient nor adequate. In addition, it held that the insecurity and vulnerability of the applicants was enormous. In conclusion, the ECtHR found that the application could not be rejected and the security forces were made responsible for the violation of the property. Therefore, among other allegations, a violation of Article 8 was given and could not be justified.

e.g.: http://www.ohchr.org/EN/HRBodies/HRC/ComplaintProcedure/Pages/HRCComplaintProcedureIndex.aspx, retrieved 30.08.2013.

Section Five:

I. International abandonment of violence against women

A. Report of the Council of Europe regarding violence against women

In July 2013, the Council of Europe published a fact-sheet concerning violence against women. Besides the commiserable fact that violence still is an unsolved matter, the report offers detailed information as to the categorization of violent acts, the alleged fundamental rights, the reasoning behind the decisions and further on the issue whether or not states are addressees to positive obligations when it comes to violent acts. Moreover, violence against women is classified as a violation of the fundamental rights and freedoms of women.

1. The facts

In daily life it seems that violence does not affect an enormous or significant number of women within Europe. Of course, situations are given where violence is observed by all of us in newspapers, television, etc but aren't we in the satisfying position of being no addresses of violence? Shouldn't we be grateful about the circumstances we are living under? The question is whether or not the appearances of these thoughts were deceptive only.

The Commission on the Status of women of the UN as well as the World Health Organization listed few, more than apprehensive, key statistics on the facts, numbers, victims and geographical conditions of violence against women:

1. Violence against women - particularly intimate partner violence and sexual violence against women - are major public health problems and violations of women's human rights.
2. Recent global prevalence figures indicate that 35% of women worldwide have experienced either intimate partner violence or non-partner sexual violence in their lifetime.
3. On average, 30% of women who have been in a relationship report that they have experienced some form of physical or sexual violence by their partner.
4. Globally, as many as 38% of murders of women are committed by an intimate partner.
5. Violence can result in physical, mental, sexual, reproductive health and other health problems, and may increase vulnerability to HIV.
6. Risk factors for being a perpetrator include low education, exposure to child maltreatment or witnessing violence in the family, harmful use of alcohol, attitudes accepting of violence and gender inequality.
7. Risk factors for being a victim of intimate partner and sexual violence include low education, witnessing violence between parents, exposure to abuse during childhood and attitudes accepting violence and gender inequality.

8. In high-income settings, school-based programs to prevent relationship violence among young people (or dating violence) are supported by some evidence of effectiveness.
9. In low-income settings, other primary prevention strategies, such as micro-finance combined with gender equality training and community-based initiatives that address gender inequality and communication and relationship skills, hold promise.
10. Situations of conflict, post conflict and displacement may exacerbate existing violence and present new forms of violence against women.[238]

2. Definition, categories and the presence of violence against women

'We must consider, however, that violence is often 'not a quality of the act the person commits, but rather a consequence of the application by others of rules and sanctions to an offender. In other words, violence is a label, and there is nothing automatic about the relation between committing a violent act and being labeled a criminal or deviant.'[239]

Clearly, this is a dogmatic and social-scientific question but generally formulated, violence is an act against another individual which affects the victim in its integrity based on a wrong-going according to particular rules. Important to notice seems the fact that violence does not only imply physical acts, but also psychological acts. Violence against women can be considered as a 'termini' which describes acts against the female sex motivated by the victims' gender.[240] The United Nations defined violence against women as 'any act of gender-based violence that results in, or is likely to

---

[238] e.g.: http://www.unric.org/en/uk-a-ireland-news-archive/28258-key-statistics-on-violence-against-women-and-girls-, retrieved 31.08.2013.
1 in 3 women have been beaten or sexually abused in her lifetime. Usually the abuser is a member of her own family or someone known to her

Boys who witness their fathers' violence are 10 times more likely to engage in spouse abuse in later adulthood

In some parts of the world a girl is more likely to be raped than to learn how to read

Every year, 60 million girls are sexually assaulted at, or on their way to, school

Women and girls are 80% (640.000) of the estimated 800,000 people trafficked across national borders annually with the majority (505.600) trafficked for sexual exploitation.

At least 60 million girls are 'missing' from various populations - mostly in Asia - as a result of infanticide, neglect or sex-selected abortions.

Up to 5% of women report being physically abused while pregnant. 50% of physically abused Indian women report violence during pregnancy

Between 100 and 140 million women and girls alive today have been subjected to Female Genital Mutilation. In six African countries over 80% of women have been subject to this practice.

http://www.who.int/mediacentre/factsheets/fs239/en/, retrieved 02.12.2013.

[239] DeKeseredy W.S., *Violence Against Women: Myths, Facts, Controversies* (2011), p. 4.

[240] e.g.: Cook R.J., *Human Rights of Women - National and International Perspectives* (1994).

result in, physical, sexual or mental harm or suffering to women, including threats of such acts, coercion or arbitrary deprivation of liberty, whether occurring in public or in private life.'[241]

There are various, obvious as well as subtle, different forms of violence, but I would like to focus on two main scopes of violence against women which are relevant at this juncture, because the following cases will mainly concern these kinds of violence; physical violence against women within the family on the one hand, and on the other hand, physical violence within the community committed by strangers.

The first one deals with violence committed by family members - domestic violence. Besides the fact that violence within the family is the most insidious form of discrimination, one of the severe reasons regarding violence against women has been identified as an outcome on the grounds of patriarchal systems and stereotypes, which are still very common within family structures.

Therefore, violent acts often derive from the subordinate positions of women in comparison to the positions of men; that phenomenon is widely spread in all societies, and not only a regional problem of specific groups.[242] Possible forms of domestic violence are, for example, sexual abuse, rape, mental and psychological abuse as well as physical abusive acts, expulsion of the children and the woman, etc. As the World Health Organization specified 'Intimate partner violence refers to behaviour by an intimate partner or ex-partner that causes physical, sexual or psychological harm, including physical aggression, sexual coercion, psychological abuse and controlling behaviours.[...]

---

241 http://www.who.int/mediacentre/factsheets/fs239/en/, retrieved 03.12.2013.

242 e.g.: http://www.un.org/womenwatch/daw/cedaw/reports.htm, retrieved 03.12.2013.
The Country Reports to the United Nations Entity for Gender Equality and the Empowerment of Women reveal the alarming and delicate situation in several States which ratified the CEDAW. For example, regarding Angola, it has been reported that 'Domestic crimes are rarely punished, and when complaints are filed and reach the courts, a great deal of leniency is always shown in sentencing the men. The traditional view that the woman is the guilty party, or provoked the assault and that the husband has the right to punish her means that many offenses are never punished.[...]Family members put a lot of pressure on women to discourage her from filing a complaint, or to get her to withdraw it if she filed one.[...]There are many cases of sexual abuse of mature women, adolescents, and even small children. But, unfortunately, because of the scant attention paid by the police and courts, it is impossible to know how many of these cases there are. Usually, the victims and their families keep silent about this problem.' An other precarious situation was observed in Albania, when the Report reads, inter alia, 'Domestic violence is still perceived in Albania as a private issue to be dealt with at family level. Thus despite a comprehensive set of rules in the Penal Code prohibiting violence (being it domestic or non-domestic) the numbers of women subject to violence is perceived to be high and goes unreported to the police, to health authorities and specific services established for this purpose.[...] Domestic violence goes mainly unreported for the following reason:
Women's perception that if they are abused is because they did something wrong; Women's distrust in the police forces and judicial system; Lack of public awareness on the fact that domestic violence represents a crime and as such it should be condemned; Lack of specific police and health structures to deal with domestic violence; Lack of awareness of the judicial system on the extent of the phenomenon and how to deal with it [...] The State does not up to now provide assistance services for cases of domestic violence, but it has supported women's associations'.'
Regarding violence against women, Austria reports, '[...] 2.514 women in Austria were the victim of rape (4% were married to or cohabited with the offender). According to the experts, the number of unrecorded cases is ten to twenty times higher. In 80% of the cases, the perpetrator and the victim had a long-term relationship or had become acquainted shortly before. Rapes by unknown men are relatively rare. The rate of acquittals after rapes (34% [...]), which is relatively high by international standards, has further risen in recent years. [...]If the panel of judges is composed only of men, the likelihood of acquittal is doubled.'

Sexual violence is any sexual act, attempt to obtain a sexual act, or other act directed against a person's sexuality using coercion, by any person regardless of their relationship to the victim, in any setting. It includes rape, defined as the physically forced or otherwise coerced penetration of the vulva or anus with a penis, other body part or object.'[243] Consequently, the physical as well as psychological autonomy and self-determination are of unbelievable importance.[244]

The second form of violence deals with the problematic of the presence within the Community as a whole. The CEDAW-Committee observed diverse forms of psychological and physical violence, e.g.: rape, gang rape, sexual assault, further different forms of violence of the community are prostitution, exploitation of prostitution, drug trafficking, pornography, trade in women, illegal migration, organized crime, etc. The Committee found that 'the repetition of such serious acts of violence over a sustained period of time constituted systematic violence founded in a culture of violence and discrimination, based upon women's alleged inferiority that has developed specific characteristics marked by hatred and misogyny and has given rise to a culture of impunity.'[245] It is outrageous that several provisions of the State's criminal law are defining rape in terms of force rather than consent, or are qualifying sexual abuse as a crime of morality than as violent crime. The Committee also requested that the authorities reflect the realities of sexual abuse which women are confronted with, further, it required a wider definition of rape.[246] As it will be apparent in the following case analyzes, the authorities are required to take effective positive measures against perpetrators in order to fulfill their duties, regrettably it seems to be more common, than figured at a first glance, to prefer acting as a passive and uninvolved, in the sense of being a non-addressee, part. Non the less, the authorities definitely are required to take actions, if any discriminatory behavior emerges. Furthermore, the State Parties are the addressees of the obligation to respect the right of women to be free from violence which, logically, includes the verification that criminal, administrative, labour and civil laws provide an efficient and adequate legal framework in order to combat such violent acts. If States deny such obligation, this results in a form of denial of the right of equality of men and women to their enjoyment of human and fundamental rights.[247]

[243] http://www.who.int/mediacentre/factsheets/fs239/en/, retrieved 03.12.2013.
[244] Freeman M.A., Rudolf B., Chinkin C., *The UN Convention on the Elimination of All Forms of Discrimination Against Women* (2012).
[245] Freeman M.A., Rudolf B., Chinkin C., *The UN Convention on the Elimination of All Forms of Discrimination Against Women* (2012), p.457.
[246] Freeman M.A., Rudolf B., Chinkin C., *The UN Convention on the Elimination of All Forms of Discrimination Against Women* (2012), p.457.
[247] e.g.: Freeman M.A., Rudolf B., Chinkin C., *The UN Convention on the Elimination of All Forms of Discrimination Against Women* (2012), p.468.

3. Cases concerning violence against women

a. Violation of Article 3 of the ECHR

In the following case the Court dealt with a case of domestic violence by her partner. The applicant repeatedly suffered from acts of violence which caused minor physical and psychological harm. When contacting the police, she got rejected without any further investigation of her complaint. She claimed that 'domestic authorities' compliance with the relevant procedural rules, as well as the manner in which the criminal-law mechanisms were implemented in the instant case as regards her complaints of attacks on her physical integrity, were insufficient to the point of constituting a violation of her rights under Articles 6 and 13 of the Convention.'[248] The Court clarified that the applicant suffered from severe physical injuries and besides the physical violence, the psychological component needed to be taken in account too, on several occasions.

The issue laid on the fact that the Lithuanian authorities did not caused the injuries, so how could they possibly be responsible for the circumstances? The Court manifested that '[...]even in the absence of any direct responsibility for the acts of a private individual under Article 3 of the Convention, State responsibility may nevertheless be engaged through the obligation imposed by Article 1 of the Convention. In this context, the Court reiterates that the obligation on the High Contracting Parties under Article 1 ECHR is to secure everyone within their jurisdiction; the rights and freedoms defined in the Convention, taken together with Article 3 ECHR, requires States to take measures designed to ensure that individuals within their jurisdiction are not subjected to torture or inhuman or degrading treatment or punishment, including such ill-treatment administered by private individuals'[249] In regard of these reasons the Court found that Lithuania should have offered sufficient protection in form of proper investigation at the first place and second, the discontinuation of an investigation is interfering with the right of Article 3 ECHR.

b. Violation of Article 8 ECHR

Aged 14 the applicant was raped by two men. In Bulgaria the age of consent is given at the age of 14. She claimed that '[...] domestic law and practice in rape cases should determine the existence, or lack, of consent to sexual intercourse on the basis of all relevant factors. In her view, a legal framework and practice that required proof of physical resistance by the victim, and thus left unpunished certain acts of rape, were inadequate.'[250] Further on she noted that if the state sets the age of consent for sexual intercourse at the age of 14, it is absolutely absurd that Bulgaria only

[248] Valielienė v. Lithuania, judgment of 26.03.2013, para. 44, ECHR.
[249] Valielienė v. Lithuania, judgment of 26.03.2013, para. 74, ECHR.
[250] M.C. v. Bulgaria, judgment of 04.12.2003, para. 111, ECHR.

prosecutes individuals who committed a rape if violent resistance by the victim has been given. Children cannot be best protected under such circumstances.

The Court held that '[...]historically, proof of physical force and physical resistance was required under domestic law and practice in rape cases in a number of countries. The last decades, however, have seen a clear and steady trend in Europe and some other parts of the world towards abandoning formalistic definitions and narrow interpretations of the law in this area. In addition to that, it noted that '[...]have agreed that penalizing non-consensual sexual acts, '[including] in cases where the victim does not show signs of resistance', is necessary for the effective protection of women against violence[...].'[251] The Court noticed that violent resistance is not necessary to qualify an sexual act as rape, because in most of the cases where children, persons with mental disorders, physical disabilities, etc. are the victims, no physical resistance was given due to physical reasons or psychological reasons but this does not lead to the conclusion that the sexual interference based on consent. The Court found violations of Article 8 ECHR and Article 3 ECHR due to the lack of legal possibilities to prosecute the perpetrators and found it detective. The domestic law does not sufficiently protect the rights of the individuals and does not offer an effective legal system.

Similar to that case was the reasoning of the Court in the I.G.-case where the Court had to examine whether or not a sufficient investigation was performed into a rape of a 14 year old girl. It held that 'The Court notes that this decision was adopted without some important investigative measures having been conducted.[...] In particular, since the central task in this case was to determine whether the sexual intercourse had been consensual, it was imperative to form an opinion concerning each party's credibility.

The Court considers that States have positive obligations inherent in Article 3 of the Convention to enact criminal law provisions effectively punishing rape and to apply them in practice through effective investigation and prosecution'[252]

---

251 M.C. v. Bulgaria, judgment of 04.12.2003, para. 162, ECHR.

252 I.G. v. Moldova, judgment of 15.05.2012, para. 42 to 43, ECHR.
The applicant was 14 at the time of the events. She joined V.R. and his friends at a bar and after being forced to drink due to mental pressure, she also took few alcoholic drinks. The claimant alleged V.R. of harassing her and by the reason of the amount of alcohol she drank, she was not able to move nor to defend herself. The defendant removed her clothes and began having sexual intercourse with her. He disputed these facts and submitted that she had immediately accepted his proposal. The ordered forensic examination verified that there had been a rupture of the hymen, but no traces of sperm or blood were found. Applications that she had been so intoxicated, logically not being able to control her actions and that he did not know about her age were rejected, respectively. The Court concluded that the sexual intercourse had been mutually consensual by the reason of the lacking signs of violence. The case was brought before the ECtHR. The applicant then concluded that her case never had been examined properly which led to a mistreatment and discrimination of her sex. The authorities in charge failed to protect her as a minor by not effectively assessing the matter of consent in regard of the entire circumstances. This was a breach of a positive obligation on the grounds of not enacting criminal law provisions. The ECtHR concluded that the examination of the circumstances and events had not been satisfying because the authorities based their conclusions solely on non-trustworthy statements, consequently the question of consent had not been sufficiently investigated. In conclusion, the Court found that the practice of the investigation concerned fell

c. Violation of Article 3 and Article 8 ECHR

In this particular case, the applicant complaint that Moldovan authorities omitted to offering a sufficient and adequate protection, although it would have been their responsibility to safeguard the applicant from the abusive and violent husband. Additionally, did their children suffer from violent acts; it also would have been the obligation of the authorities to offer them protection. The claimant stated that they were infringed in their right to live without inhuman and degrading treatment and that their right for private and family life.

The Court summarized that 'The first applicant argued that the State had failed to discharge its positive obligation under Article 3 of the Convention to protect her from domestic violence and to prevent the recurrence of such violence. She was a particularly vulnerable person since her aggressor was a police officer and had the support of his colleagues and other local authorities, which made her attempts to obtain protection more difficult.' [253] Clearly, the Court did not question the relevant record; analyzes whether or not the authorities violated their obligations in form of negating their obligations to act and if so, if the requirements were fulfilled regarding particular passages. The question arose if the ill-treatment of her could be classified as an ill-treatment.

'[...]it depends on all the circumstances of the case, such as the nature and context of the treatment, its duration, its physical and mental effects and, in some instances, the sex, age and state of health of the victim'[254]. Without doubt, the violation the victims suffered from such extreme, intense and brutal dimensions; this does not require a deeper investigation.

Although it is not the Courts' responsibility to replace any national function regarding matters like the decision 'which possible' and 'what kind' of measures could have been taken to act in accordance with the ECHR. The inherent character of the effectiveness of the rights demands that the Court is in charge of examining whether or not the authorities actions were properly chosen and if the official investigations reached up to the ECHRs' requirements. It noted that 'States are to maintain and apply in practice an adequate legal framework affording protection against acts of violence by private individuals.[...]the Moldovan law provided for specific criminal sanctions for committing acts of violence against members of one's own family. Moreover, the law provided for protective measures for the victims of family violence, as well as for sanctions against those persons who refused to abide by court decisions. The Court concludes that the authorities had put in place a legislative framework allowing them to take measures against persons accused of family violence.'[255] The authorities were well informed and evidently aware of the ongoing domestic violence against the applicant. The accused husband returned to their home, although being ad-

---

short of the requirements inherent in the Member's positive obligations regarding sexual abuse and rape. Consequently Moldova breached Article 3 of the Convention.

[253] Eremia v. the Republic of Moldova, judgment of 28.05.2013, para. 40, ECHR.

[254] Eremia v. the Republic of Moldova, judgment of 28.05.2013, para. 48, ECHR.

[255] Eremia v. the Republic of Moldova, judgment of 28.05.2013, para. 52 and 57, ECHR.

dressee of a protection order, where he kept on threatening the life of the applicant in the presence of their children. The authorities still remained passive. The Ministry of Internal Affairs solely issued a warning. 'The absence of decisive action by the authorities in dealing with A. is even more disturbing considering that the aggressor was a police officer whose professional requirements included, under domestic law[...], the protection of the rights of others, the prevention of crime and the protection of public order.'[256]

The Court considered it as an entirely absurd approach, especially in regard of the facts that the aggressor himself was a police officer and, in addition to that, the circumstances of his violent behavior were well known. In respect of the knowledge of endangering the applicant and her children due to the repeating domestic violence, the authorities clearly disregarded their obligation to take effective measures against the aggressor. Consequently, a violation of Article 3 ECHR cannot be denied. Regarding Article 8 ECHR, the Court held that the respect of private life does include the physical and psychological integrity. The Court also found that the State is in duty to guarantee protection when the integrity is endangered, irrelevant whether the danger arises from themselves or from other individuals amongst each other. The repeatedly witnessing of the violent acts against the applicant definitely endangered the psychological health of the children. Moreover, the Court found a violation of Article 14 ECHR. 'The applicants claimed that the authorities had failed to take appropriate action aimed at preventing domestic violence, protecting from its effects, investigating the complaints and punishing the perpetrator. They thus promoted further violence from A., who felt immune to any State action. The violence was gender-based and amounted to discrimination contrary to Article 14 of the Convention.'[257] Regarding the gender targeted abuse the Court referred to the CEDAW[258] when arguing that 'If it was to be effectively tackled, such

---

[256] Eremia v. the Republic of Moldova, judgment of 28.05.2013, para. 63, ECHR.
[257] Eremia v. the Republic of Moldova, judgment of 28.05.2013, para. 82, ECHR.
[258] Freeman M.A., Rudolf B., Chinkin C., *The UN Convention On The Elimination of All Forms of Discrimination Against Women (2012):* The Convention on the Elimination of Discrimination Against Women is a wide ranging treaty which covers more than only political and economical rights, but also civil, cultural and societal fundamentally guaranteed rights. It entered into force on September the 3rd of 1981 and by now, 187 States are Parties to the treaty. The main focus laid on the fact that women should not only be protected within the public sphere, moreover they should also be protected within the private area. More than noteworthy is the fact that the CEDAW is the major instrument addressing women's fundamental rights exclusively. Further, the CEDAW could be seen as the living internationally recognized instrument in order to maintain the human rights progress, although several States made reservations, further declarations or even objections. Within the treaty a definition of discrimination had been articulated which defines the term in Article 1 of the document as following; For the purposes of the present Convention, the term "discrimination against women" shall mean any distinction, exclusion or restriction made on the basis of sex which has the effect or purpose of impairing or nullifying the recognition, enjoyment or exercise by women, irrespective of their marital status, on a basis of equality of men and women, of human rights and fundamental freedoms in the political, economic, social, cultural, civil or any other field. The Members who ratified the document are required to ensure that gender equality finds its way into the national legislation as well as administration. Further on, it states that the Members are responsible enacting provisions in order to combat any discrimination based on the sex. Furthermore, Article 2 of the treaty requires that tribunals and institutions are established to entrench effective and accurate jurisdictional possibilities to investigate and charge discriminational acts.
e.g.: Madhavi S., *Piercing the Veil,* Yale Law Journal, Volume 112/8, June 2003, pp. 1425 - 1426.

violence demanded a particular response, which included treating such violence as a form of gender-based discrimination. Failing to realize this amounted to a failure to acknowledging the magnitude of the problem and its impact upon the dignity of women. They referred to the General Recommendation No. 28 on the Core Obligations of States Parties under Article 2 of the Convention on the Elimination of All Forms of Discrimination against Women adopted by the Committee on the Elimination of Discrimination against Women (CEDAW/C/2010/47/GC.2), in accordance with which 'States parties have a due diligence obligation to prevent, investigate, prosecute and punish ... acts of gender based violence'.'[259] Obviously, the State did not only neglect its duties but also omitted to prevent its citizens from violence, which solely was motivated by gender discrimination. The applicant was permanent beaten up by her husband and the knowledge about those particular circumstances would have been to investigate and take measures. The neglecting of the authorities can be classified as a discriminatory attitude.[260]

II. Excursus: Cases concerning the private life of women

A. General questions in respect of the right to life

The right to life did not need to be created but only protected. It is substantial and self-evident to human-rights reasoning although still not clearly recognizable what scope should have been concealed. As Torkel Opsahl invoked 'When the general clause was added, it appears to be entered not as part of the definition of rights but rather in order to have a more complete enumeration.[...] its intended or potential scope still remains open[...].'[261] The most discussed matters regarding the right to life are the medical procedure of abortion, regarding the question 'When does life begin?', the question of 'When does life end?'. Furthermore, the question arose 'Which positive and negative obligations encounter the State?' Although being a self-evident right the margin of appreciation also yields its impact in such an ostensible provision. In some States contraception is still valued as an issue of the right of life and not as an artificial method of birth control. In general contraception does not affect the right of life because it finds its roots in religious and moral issues. Regarding an abortion, if it is forced there is no need to analyze it under Article 2 ECHR as it clearly contravenes against Article 8 ECHR and Article 12 ECHR. The definition of protection of life changed radically within the last decades. The fact that abortion is not forbidden in general made it more difficult to find a definition. More likely, the categorical questions of 'What is the time-limitation?', 'Who is allowed to decide?', 'On what reasons has the decision to be made?' and 'What are the sources of information for the decision?' need to be answered specifically. The

---

Cook R.J., *Human Rights of Women - National and International Perspectives* (1994).

[259] Eremia v. the Republic of Moldova, judgment of 28.05.2013, para. 84, ECHR.

[260] e.g.: Eremia v. the Republic of Moldova, judgment of 28.05.2013.

[261] Torkel Opsahl in *The European System for the Protection of Human Rights* (1993), *p.208.*

interpretation of Article 2 ECHR seems more realistic if it is accepted that the protection of an unborn life is more relative than that of a person after birth but yet there is no consensus in terms of an exact definition and thus an universally valid protection has not been found. The question 'Is a potential father an indirect victim comparatively to a woman as direct victim?' was brought up.

1. The protection of life versus the right to private life

As related to these questions, the most significant decisions were X v. United Kingdom [262] and Vo v. France [263]. On the one hand there is the need to protect the life of each individual and on the other hand, the right to private life needs to be respected. The following cases will demonstrate the difficulty and challenge if it comes to the situation, where a decision has to be made between the two rights mentioned above. In the former case a husband complained because no rights were recognized regarding him as indirect victim in case of an abortion. His wife had an abortion without his consent. The Court manifested that there is no such absolute right of a fetus when the carrying on the pregnancy could possibly endanger the life of the woman. It declared that there is no need for any other clarification which means that indirect it denied the proposal. In the latter the claimant accused France of a lacking protection of the fetus while having a medical procedure. The medical treatment of the claimant was unsuccessful and major mistakes have been made in the hospital. The pregnancy was too risky for continuation and was terminated on reasons of health.[264]

The alleged violation of Article 2 ECHR because of an unintentional homicide, although allowing abortions in certain cases, was refused. The Court held that every person is protected, but the right of life of an unborn is limited when endangering the mother's life. The Court also clarified that a balance needs to be found between medical, ethical, moral, legal and cultural aspects in terms of defining a 'human being'. To ensure that balance , justified with the instrument of margin of appreciation, it obliges every State to implement certain cultural, ethical, moral or philosophical aspects through defining specific facts, phrases or circumstances. By virtue of such nationally

---

[262] X v. United Kingdom, judgment of 05.11.1981, ECHR.

[263] Vo v. France, judgment of 08.07.2004, ECHR.

e.g.: Airey v. Ireland, judgment of 09.10.1979, ECHR.

Tysiac v. Poland,judgment of 20.03.2007, ECHR.

The case was brought to the ECtHR by a pregnant woman who suffered from severe myopia. She gained a certificate referring to her medical condition. The certificate attested that the pregnancy, bedsides already raising two little children, was a threat to her health, subsequently, these medical considerations led to the result that a termination of the pregnancy would be lawfully. She underwent further medical examinations, apparently the doctor in charge declared the pregnancy not to be threatening. Thus, the claimant did not decide to terminate the pregnancy. After giving birth to the third child her eyesight deteriorated significantly. According to the Law on family planning a termination of a pregnancy was lawful under certain circumstanc-es, e.g.: if it is endangering the mother's life, if the termination was not based on these reasons, the persons were accused of criminal offences. The claimant filed a complaint by the reason of violation of Article 3 of the Convention; in specific, that no one shall be subjected to...inhuman or degrading treatment. The Court found that there was no breach of Article 3 by the reason of not offering appropriate medical treatment y the Contracting State. Further charges were made regarding Article 8 of the Convention.

[264] e.g.: Janis M., Kay R., Bradley A., *European Human Rights Law* (2008), p. 121.

individual definitions and the following implementation of these in the constitutional or statutory basis it becomes a considerably and inescapably fact when it comes to a judgment of the ECtHR. Although respecting the margin of appreciation in the Case of A,B,C v. Ireland [265] the Court verified an accusation in one of the three cases. The women all alleged violations because of the prohibition of an abortion, although the continuance of the pregnancy was endangering their life. 'That interference had been in accordance with the law and had pursued the legitimate aim of protecting public morals as understood in Ireland.'[266] The Court only recognized a violation of Article 8 ECHR in the case of C. She was suffering from cancer before and the pregnancy was seriously threatening her life and it contravenes with the respect of her privacy. Due to of the lacking consensus there is no clear status of an embryo. The Court and the Commission repeatedly announced that a plausible definition cannot be made. E.g. '[...]not likely to make categorial findings as to whether, for instance, 'fetus life' is or is not 'human life'. Perhaps the criterion of viability may be seen as the definitive beginning point of such life as must nor be intentionally taken, unless other life (the mother´s) is endangered. Another possibility would be to establish procedural guarantees without constructing it as a subjective right. [267]

2. Protection of Life During Pregnancy Act 2013

This case probably would lead to divergent decisions in 2013 because of the implementation of the Protection of Life During Pregnancy Act 2013. A new legislation allows the determination in specific cases as these are serious risk of loss of life or suicidal tendency. Because of the margin of appreciation the Court needs to consider the newly enforced Bill while deciding on a case. Except for formal restrictions; the fact that two medical practitioners jointly need to certify the material requirements for a legal abortion, the consulting mechanism needs to be complied, the material restrictions need to be fulfilled. The criterion for an abortion are the risk of loss of life from physical illness, the risk of being self destructive as quoted in Head 2 of the Act, where it says '[...] there is a real and substantial risk of loss of the pregnant woman's life other than by way of self-destruction' [...] Essentially, the decision to be reached is not so much a balancing of the competing rights- rather, it is a clinical assessment as to whether the mother's life, as opposed to her health, is threatened by a real and substantial risk that can only be averted by a termination of pregnancy.[268] Yet not decidedly quoted are cases of rape or incest. Women who seek for a termination because the continuation of the pregnancy would be mortal for the fetus are not explicitly mentioned in the Act. This means that a woman, who is a victim of one of these two crimes, still, cannot seek a legal

---

[265] A,B,C v. Ireland, judgment of 16.12.2010, ECHR.
[266] Roca J.G., Santolaya P., *Europe of Rights: A compendium on the European Convention of Human Rights* (2008), p.57.
[267] Torkel Opsahl in *The European System for the Protection of Human Rights* (1993), p.221.
[268] Protection of Life During Pregnancy Act 2013 combined with explanatory notes.

termination but in case of physical illness or self destructive danger. Preeminent is the fact that in the explanatory notes the decisions of A,B,C v Ireland[269] and Tysiąc v Poland[270] are mentioned and as result of the circumstances back then in correspondence with the argumentation of the ECtHR the review of medical procedures have to satisfy through containing specific attributes; for example, independence, competence to review the medical history and decision, timely drawn decisions, all opinions need to be written. Summarized, it has to be said that the effectiveness and application of the Act, first of all clearly, depends on the medical investigation and interpretation of the term 'substantial risk of loss of life'. Moreover, besides clear definitions and medical indication, in terms of accepted, obvious risks which will not stand any expandable interpretation whether there is or is not a fatal risk. Finally, the Court has the obligation to draw a decision. It is not clear yet, how the national courts will interpret the Act, if it comes to specific not defined matters. Additionally, it has to be noted that women who are pregnant because of rape or incest are not considered; also the fact that a fetus may not be viable if continuing the pregnancy although applying all medical possibilities is still not clarified regarding legal terms. Clearly, the intent behind the Act seems not to be the legalization of abortion in a wider spread sense and change of moral view but to stop the 'abortion trail' to Great Britain. Another question is the weight and balance of the arguments within the requirements of a legal abortion. If the Act should protect the women's life, does the fact that a raped woman still need to suffer from a serious risk of loss of life or suicidal tendency implies protection? Regarding the European sphere it depends on whether or not the Court inclines to a narrow interpretation of the Act especially considering the margin of appreciation. [271]

[269] A,B,C v Ireland, judgment of 16.12.2010, ECHR.
[270] Tysiąc v Poland, judgment of 20.03.2007, ECHR.
[271] Protection of Life During Pregnancy Act 2013, Number 35 of 2013. http://www.theguardian.com/world/2013/jul/30/abortion-ireland-becomes-legal-circumstances, retrieved 20.08.2013.

Section Six:

I. Closing Remarks

I would like to cite Janis Mark W.; 'In many ways, it is already a remarkable triumph. Sitting the apex of the most successful international legal regime for the protection of human rights, the European Court of Human Rights has generated, as we have seen, a remarkable jurisprudence, having rendered hundreds of judgments about a wide range of specific substantive human rights.'[272] Indeed, the process of human rights development is astonishing and remarkable. The implementation of Human Rights Law into the European legal system is of unbelievable significance and importance. Not to mention, the fact that this progress has been made within a few decades. Moreover, the developed system to protect human rights has led to an enormous impact on the legal systems of the Member States. The national Courts have been forced to re-arrange their national legal behavior; re-consider their national legal system. The administrative powers have been pushed to reflect whether or not certain morals and regulations are stainable. Is the protection of fundamental rights guaranteed in a sufficient manner? Indeed, the analyzed cases offered an insight, due to that, it is evident that human rights protection lacks from a sufficient implementation and application. On the one hand, there are the interests of the concerning States; political, economical and social interests, which still seem to be of high importance to the administrative organs. Consequently, the protection of fundamental rights is treated subsidiary in particular situations. States are aware of their power, like the analyzed cases revealed; the Member States often base their argumentation on sovereignty. The urgent need of specific regulations and administrative behavior is repeatedly argued by the States. One could ask, is the protection guaranteed if States evidently want to keep the current national system alive? The judgments showed the difficult process, when it comes to the application of particular methods; like the margin of appreciation. The Court needs to weigh the interests and enter total new territory regarding certain questions. Without question, the created system of the judicial process has been necessary to establish the ECHR. This system also brought up its own difficulties; e.g. setting a narrower or less narrow margin of appreciation, judging in accordance with the social development, respecting the change of meanings of circumstances, etc. Probably, the European thought of sovereignty has been and will be a huge challenge regarding a sufficient protection.[273]

On the other hand, the Court has to find a balance between the protection of individuals and the States. The Court needs to define specific circumstances, which are unclear. Europe is multicultural, therefore, the responsibility in order to find adequate solutions to unclear situations or 'phrases' is more than difficult. The judgments have to cover the different legal understanding and the different

[272] Janis M.W., Kay R.S., Bradley A.W., *European Human Rights Law,* (2008), p.878.
[273] e.g.: Janis M.W., Kay R.S., Bradley A.W., *European Human Rights Law,* (2008).

needs of individuals and States. Besides that, the European Court of Human Rights has created its own specific difficulties. Strasbourg is fighting with the amount of cases. This leads to the effect, that the Court struggles to generate adequate and well considered judgments. Moreover, the coverage of certain fundamental rights is still not clarified. Particular rights remain unprotected within the Strasbourg system. Furthermore, instances of non-compliance are still troubling a sufficient protection of human rights. Consequently, new mechanisms need to be found, if Strasbourg wants to offer an adequate protection. One option is to combine the Strasbourg organs with the European Union institutions. The question is, if there are two systems, why not combining them? The workload of the Strasbourg machinery is too much to carry; hence, is it too ambitious for the Court to cover more cases? This clearly affects the quality of the judgments. Logically, the protection of fundamental rights won't be guaranteed in a sufficient manner. Due to that problem, the question is, whether or not, to add the European Union institutions regarding human rights matters; or is it the Strasbourg machinery, which simply needs to be extended in other forms? Of course, Strasbourg did not generate these difficulties only by itself. In addition to the existing problems, the States make their contribution; if ignoring structural problems. The Court clearly announced that, it would be much easier, if the States would follow a proportionate implementation of the Strasbourg judgments. The problem of non-compliance could be solved easier. Another question is, if the European Court of Human Rights should become a Supreme Constitutional Court? Finally, one can say, that many questions have been answered within the decades and many questions arose through the case-law of the European Court of Human Rights. Obviously, human rights protection remains an issue with many difficulties.[274]

[274] e.g.: Janis M.W., Kay R.S., Bradley A.W., *European Human Rights Law,* (2008).

II. Appendix

A. Universal Declaration of Human Rights

On December 10, 1948 the General Assembly of the United Nations adopted and proclaimed the Universal Declaration of Human Rights the full text of which appears in the following pages. Following this historic act the Assembly called upon all Member countries to publicize the text of the Declaration and "to cause it to be disseminated, displayed, read and expounded principally in schools and other educational institutions, without distinction based on the political status of countries or territories."

PREAMBLE

Whereas recognition of the inherent dignity and of the equal and inalienable rights of all members of the human family is the foundation of freedom, justice and peace in the world,

Whereas disregard and contempt for human rights have resulted in barbarous acts which have outraged the conscience of mankind, and the advent of a world in which human beings shall enjoy freedom of speech and belief and freedom from fear and want has been proclaimed as the highest aspiration of the common people,

Whereas it is essential, if man is not to be compelled to have recourse, as a last resort, to rebellion against tyranny and oppression, that human rights should be protected by the rule of law,

Whereas it is essential to promote the development of friendly relations between nations,

Whereas the peoples of the United Nations have in the Charter reaffirmed their faith in fundamental human rights, in the dignity and worth of the human person and in the equal rights of men and women and have determined to promote social progress and better standards of life in larger freedom,

Whereas Member States have pledged themselves to achieve, in co-operation with the United Nations, the promotion of universal respect for and observance of human rights and fundamental freedoms,

Whereas a common understanding of these rights and freedoms is of the greatest importance for the full realization of this pledge,

Now, Therefore,

THE GENERAL ASSEMBLY

proclaims

THIS UNIVERSAL DECLARATION OF HUMAN RIGHTS as a common standard of achievement for all peoples and all nations, to the end that every individual and every organ of society, keeping this Declaration constantly in mind, shall strive by teaching and education to promote respect for these rights and freedoms and by progressive measures, national and international, to secure their universal and effective recognition and observance, both among the peoples of Member States themselves and among the peoples of territories under their jurisdiction.

Article 7

All are equal before the law and are entitled without any discrimination to equal protection of the law. All are entitled to equal protection against any discrimination in violation of this Declaration and against any incitement to such discrimination.

Article 24

Everyone has the right to rest and leisure, including reasonable limitation of working hours and periodic holidays with pay.

B. The Charter of the United Nations

Article 7

1. There are established as principal organs of the United Nations: a General Assembly, a Security Council, an Economic and Social Council, a Trusteeship Council, an International Court of Justice and a Secretariat.
2. Such subsidiary organs as may be found necessary may be established in accordance with the present Charter.

Article 24

1. In order to ensure prompt and effective action by the United Nations, its Members confer on the Security Council primary responsibility for the maintenance of international peace and security, and agree that in carrying out its duties under this responsibility the Security Council acts on their behalf.
2. In discharging these duties the Security Council shall act in accordance with the Purposes and Principles of the United Nations. The specific powers granted to the Security Council for the discharge of these duties are laid down in Chapters VI, VII, VIII, and XII.
3. The Security Council shall submit annual and, when necessary, special reports to the General Assembly for its consideration.

Article 92

The International Court of Justice shall be the principal judicial organ of the United Nations. It shall function in accordance with the annexed Statute, which is based upon the Statute of the Permanent Court of International Justice and forms an integral part of the present Charter.

C. Statutes of the ICJ

Article 38

1. The Court, whose function is to decide in accordance with international law such disputes as are submitted to it, shall apply:

a. international conventions, whether general or particular, establishing rules expressly recognized by the contesting states;

b. international custom, as evidence of a general practice accepted as law;

c. the general principles of law recognized by civilized nations;

d. subject to the provisions of Article 59, judicial decisions and the teachings of the most highly qualified publicists of the various nations, as subsidiary means for the determination of rules of law.

2. This provision shall not prejudice the power of the Court to decide a case ex aequo et bono, if the parties agree thereto.

D. Convention for the Protection of Human Rights and Fundamental Freedoms as amended by Protocols No. 11 and No. 14.

The governments signatory hereto, being members of the Council of Europe,

Considering the Universal Declaration of Human Rights proclaimed by the General Assembly of the United Nations on 10th December 1948;

Considering that this Declaration aims at securing the universal and effective recognition and observance of the Rights therein declared;

Considering that the aim of the Council of Europe is the achievement of greater unity between its members and that one of the methods by which that aim is to be pursued is the maintenance and further realisation of human rights and fundamental freedoms;

Reaffirming their profound belief in those fundamental freedoms which are the foundation of justice and peace in the world and are best maintained on the one hand by an effective political democracy and on the other by a common understanding and observance of the human rights upon which they depend;

Being resolved, as the governments of European countries which are like-minded and have a common heritage of political traditions, ideals, freedom and the rule of law, to take the first steps for the collective enforcement of certain of the rights stated in the Universal Declaration,

Have agreed as follows:

Article 1 – Obligation to respect human rights

The High Contracting Parties shall secure to everyone within their jurisdiction the rights and freedoms defined in Section I of this Convention.

Section I – Rights and freedoms

Article 2 – Right to life

1. Everyone's right to life shall be protected by law. No one shall be deprived of his life intentionally save in the execution of a sentence of a court following his conviction of a crime for which this penalty is provided by law.
2. Deprivation of life shall not be regarded as inflicted in contravention of this article when it results from the use of force which is no more than absolutely necessary:

a. in defence of any person from unlawful violence;
b. in order to effect a lawful arrest or to prevent the escape of a person lawfully detained;
c. in action lawfully taken for the purpose of quelling a riot or insurrection.

Article 3 – Prohibition of torture

No one shall be subjected to torture or to inhuman or degrading treatment or punishment.

Article 4 – Prohibition of slavery and forced labour

1. No one shall be held in slavery or servitude.
2. No one shall be required to perform forced or compulsory labour.
3. For the purpose of this article the term "forced or compulsory labour" shall not include:
   a. any work required to be done in the ordinary course of detention imposed according to the provisions of Article 5 of this Convention or during conditional release from such detention;
   b. any service of a military character or, in case of conscientious objectors in countries where they are recognised, service exacted instead of compulsory military service;
   c. any service exacted in case of an emergency or calamity threatening the life or well-being of the community;
   d. any work or service which forms part of normal civic obligations.

Article 5 – Right to liberty and security

1. Everyone has the right to liberty and security of person. No one shall be deprived of his liberty save in the following cases and in accordance with a procedure prescribed by law:
   a. the lawful detention of a person after conviction by a competent court;
   b. the lawful arrest or detention of a person for non-compliance with the lawful order of a court or in order to secure the fulfilment of any obligation prescribed by law;
   c. the lawful arrest or detention of a person effected for the purpose of bringing him before the competent legal authority on reasonable suspicion of having committed an offence or when it is reasonably considered necessary to prevent his committing an offence or fleeing after having done so;
   d. the detention of a minor by lawful order for the purpose of educational supervision or his lawful detention for the purpose of bringing him before the competent legal authority;

e. the lawful detention of persons for the prevention of the spreading of infectious diseases, of persons of unsound mind, alcoholics or drug addicts or vagrants;
f. the lawful arrest or detention of a person to prevent his effecting an unauthorised entry into the country or of a person against whom action is being taken with a view to deportation or extradition.

2. Everyone who is arrested shall be informed promptly, in a language which he understands, of the reasons for his arrest and of any charge against him.
3. Everyone arrested or detained in accordance with the provisions of paragraph 1.c of this article shall be brought promptly before a judge or other officer authorised by law to exercise judicial power and shall be entitled to trial within a reasonable time or to release pending trial. Release may be conditioned by guarantees to appear for trial.
4. Everyone who is deprived of his liberty by arrest or detention shall be entitled to take proceedings by which the lawfulness of his detention shall be decided speedily by a court and his release ordered if the detention is not lawful.
5. Everyone who has been the victim of arrest or detention in contravention of the provisions of this article shall have an enforceable right to compensation.

Article 6 – Right to a fair trial

1. In the determination of his civil rights and obligations or of any criminal charge against him, everyone is entitled to a fair and public hearing within a reasonable time by an independent and impartial tribunal established by law. Judgment shall be pronounced publicly but the press and public may be excluded from all or part of the trial in the interests of morals, public order or national security in a democratic society, where the interests of juveniles or the protection of the private life of the parties so require, or to the extent strictly necessary in the opinion of the court in special circumstances where publicity would prejudice the interests of justice.
2. Everyone charged with a criminal offence shall be presumed innocent until proved guilty according to law.
3. Everyone charged with a criminal offence has the following minimum rights:
   a. to be informed promptly, in a language which he understands and in detail, of the nature and cause of the accusation against him;
   b. to have adequate time and facilities for the preparation of his defence;
   c. to defend himself in person or through legal assistance of his own choosing or, if he has not sufficient means to pay for legal assistance, to be given it free when the interests of justice so require;

d. to examine or have examined witnesses against him and to obtain the attendance and examination of witnesses on his behalf under the same conditions as witnesses against him;
e. to have the free assistance of an interpreter if he cannot understand or speak the language used in court.

Article 7 – No punishment without law

1. No one shall be held guilty of any criminal offence on account of any act or omission which did not constitute a criminal offence under national or international law at the time when it was committed. Nor shall a heavier penalty be imposed than the one that was applicable at the time the criminal offence was committed.
2. This article shall not prejudice the trial and punishment of any person for any act or omission which, at the time when it was committed, was criminal according to the general principles of law recognised by civilised nations.

Article 8 – Right to respect for private and family life

1. Everyone has the right to respect for his private and family life, his home and his correspondence.
2. There shall be no interference by a public authority with the exercise of this right except such as is in accordance with the law and is necessary in a democratic society in the interests of national security, public safety or the economic well-being of the country, for the prevention of disorder or crime, for the protection of health or morals, or for the protection of the rights and freedoms of others.

Article 9 – Freedom of thought, conscience and religion

1. Everyone has the right to freedom of thought, conscience and religion; this right includes freedom to change his religion or belief and freedom, either alone or in community with others and in public or private, to manifest his religion or belief, in worship, teaching, practice and observance.
2. Freedom to manifest one's religion or beliefs shall be subject only to such limitations as are prescribed by law and are necessary in a democratic society in the interests of public safety, for the protection of public order, health or morals, or for the protection of the rights and freedoms of others.

Article 10 – Freedom of expression

1. Everyone has the right to freedom of expression. This right shall include freedom to hold opinions and to receive and impart information and ideas without interference by public authority and regardless of frontiers. This article shall not prevent States from requiring the licensing of broadcasting, television or cinema enterprises.
2. The exercise of these freedoms, since it carries with it duties and responsibilities, may be subject to such formalities, conditions, restrictions or penalties as are prescribed by law and are necessary in a democratic society, in the interests of national security, territorial integrity or public safety, for the prevention of disorder or crime, for the protection of health or morals, for the protection of the reputation or rights of others, for preventing the disclosure of information received in confidence, or for maintaining the authority and impartiality of the judiciary.

Article 11 – Freedom of assembly and association

1. Everyone has the right to freedom of peaceful assembly and to freedom of association with others, including the right to form and to join trade unions for the protection of his interests.
2. No restrictions shall be placed on the exercise of these rights other than such as are prescribed by law and are necessary in a democratic society in the interests of national security or public safety, for the prevention of disorder or crime, for the protection of health or morals or for the protection of the rights and freedoms of others. This article shall not prevent the imposition of lawful restrictions on the exercise of these rights by members of the armed forces, of the police or of the administration of the State.

Article 12 – Right to marry

Men and women of marriageable age have the right to marry and to found a family, according to the national laws governing the exercise of this right.

Article 13 – Right to an effective remedy

Everyone whose rights and freedoms as set forth in this Convention are violated shall have an effective remedy before a national authority notwithstanding that the violation has been committed by persons acting in an official capacity.

Article 14 – Prohibition of discrimination

The enjoyment of the rights and freedoms set forth in this Convention shall be secured without discrimination on any ground such as sex, race, colour, language, religion, political or other opinion, national or social origin, association with a national minority, property, birth or other status.

Article 15 – Derogation in time of emergency

1. In time of war or other public emergency threatening the life of the nation any High Contracting Party may take measures derogating from its obligations under this Convention to the extent strictly required by the exigencies of the situation, provided that such measures are not inconsistent with its other obligations under international law.
2. No derogation from Article 2, except in respect of deaths resulting from lawful acts of war, or from Articles 3, 4 (paragraph 1) and 7 shall be made under this provision.
3. Any High Contracting Party availing itself of this right of derogation shall keep the Secretary General of the Council of Europe fully informed of the measures which it has taken and the reasons therefor. It shall also inform the Secretary General of the Council of Europe when such measures have ceased to operate and the provisions of the Convention are again being fully executed.

Article 16 – Restrictions on political activity of aliens

Nothing in Articles 10, 11 and 14 shall be regarded as preventing the High Contracting Parties from imposing restrictions on the political activity of aliens.

Article 17 – Prohibition of abuse of rights

Nothing in this Convention may be interpreted as implying for any State, group or person any right to engage in any activity or perform any act aimed at the destruction of any of the rights and freedoms set forth herein or at their limitation to a greater extent than is provided for in the Convention.

Article 18 – Limitation on use of restrictions on rights

The restrictions permitted under this Convention to the said rights and freedoms shall not be applied for any purpose other than those for which they have been prescribed.

Section II – European Court of Human Rights

Article 19 – Establishment of the Court

To ensure the observance of the engagements undertaken by the High Contracting Parties in the Convention and the Protocols thereto, there shall be set up a European Court of Human Rights, hereinafter referred to as "the Court". It shall function on a permanent basis.

Article 20 – Number of judges

The Court shall consist of a number of judges equal to that of the High Contracting Parties.

Article 21 – Criteria for office

1. The judges shall be of high moral character and must either possess the qualifications required for appointment to high judicial office or be jurisconsults of recognised competence.
2. The judges shall sit on the Court in their individual capacity.
3. During their term of office the judges shall not engage in any activity which is incompatible with their independence, impartiality or with the demands of a full-time office; all questions arising from the application of this paragraph shall be decided by the Court.

Article 22 – Election of judges

The judges shall be elected by the Parliamentary Assembly with respect to each High Contracting Party by a majority of votes cast from a list of three candidates nominated by the High Contracting Party.

Article 23 – Terms of office and dismissal

1. The judges shall be elected for a period of nine years. They may not be re-elected.
2. The terms of office of judges shall expire when they reach the age of 70.
3. The judges shall hold office until replaced. They shall, however, continue to deal with such cases as they already have under consideration.
4. No judge may be dismissed from office unless the other judges decide by a majority of two-thirds that that judge has ceased to fulfil the required conditions.

Article 24 – Registry and rapporteurs

1. The Court shall have a registry, the functions and organisation of which shall be laid down in the rules of the Court.
2. When sitting in a single-judge formation, the Court shall be assisted by rapporteurs who shall function under the authority of the President of the Court. They shall form part of the Court's registry.

Article 25 – Plenary Court

The plenary Court shall

a. elect its President and one or two Vice-Presidents for a period of three years; they may be re-elected;
b. set up Chambers, constituted for a fixed period of time;
c. elect the Presidents of the Chambers of the Court; they may be re-elected;
d. adopt the rules of the Court;
e. elect the Registrar and one or more Deputy Registrars;
f. make any request under Article 26, paragraph 2.

Article 26 – Single-judge formation, committees, Chambers and Grand Chamber

1. To consider cases brought before it, the Court shall sit in a single-judge formation, in committees of three judges, in Chambers of seven judges and in a Grand Chamber of seventeen judges. The Court's Chambers shall set up committees for a fixed period of time.
2. At the request of the plenary Court, the Committee of Ministers may, by a unanimous decision and for a fixed period, reduce to five the number of judges of the Chambers.
3. When sitting as a single judge, a judge shall not examine any application against the High Contracting Party in respect of which that judge has been elected.
4. There shall sit as an ex officio member of the Chamber and the Grand Chamber the judge elected in respect of the High Contracting Party concerned. If there is none or if that judge is unable to sit, a person chosen by the President of the Court from a list submitted in advance by that Party shall sit in the capacity of judge.
5. The Grand Chamber shall also include the President of the Court, the Vice-Presidents, the Presidents of the Chambers and other judges chosen in accordance with the rules of the Court. When a case is referred to the Grand Chamber under Article 43, no judge from the Chamber which rendered the judgment shall sit in the Grand Chamber, with the exception of

the President of the Chamber and the judge who sat in respect of the High Contracting Party concerned.

Article 27 – Competence of single judges

1. A single judge may declare inadmissible or strike out of the Court's list of cases an application submitted under Article 34, where such a decision can be taken without further examination.
2. The decision shall be final.
3. If the single judge does not declare an application inadmissible or strike it out, that judge **shall forward it to a committee or to a Chamber for further examination.**

Article 28 – Competence of committees

1. In respect of an application submitted under Article 34, a committee may, by a unanimous vote,
   a. declare it inadmissible or strike it out of its list of cases, where such decision can be taken without further examination; or
   b. declare it admissible and render at the same time a judgment on the merits, if the underlying question in the case, concerning the interpretation or the application of the Convention or the Protocols thereto, is already the subject of well-established case-law of the Court.
2. Decisions and judgments under paragraph 1 shall be final.
3. If the judge elected in respect of the High Contracting Party concerned is not a member of the committee, the committee may at any stage of the proceedings invite that judge to take the place of one of the members of the committee, having regard to all relevant factors, including whether that Party has contested the application of the procedure under paragraph 1.b.

Article 29 – Decisions by Chambers on admissibility and merits

1. If no decision is taken under Article 27 or 28, or no judgment rendered under Article 28, a Chamber shall decide on the admissibility and merits of individual applications submitted under Article 34. The decision on admissibility may be taken separately.
2. A Chamber shall decide on the admissibility and merits of inter-State applications submitted under Article 33. The decision on admissibility shall be taken separately unless the Court, in exceptional cases, decides otherwise.

Article 30 – Relinquishment of jurisdiction to the Grand Chamber

Where a case pending before a Chamber raises a serious question affecting the interpretation of the Convention or the protocols thereto, or where the resolution of a question before the Chamber might have a result inconsistent with a judgment previously delivered by the Court, the Chamber may, at any time before it has rendered its judgment, relinquish jurisdiction in favour of the Grand Chamber, unless one of the parties to the case objects.

Article 31 – Powers of the Grand Chamber

The Grand Chamber shall:

a. determine applications submitted either under Article 33 or Article 34 when a Chamber has relinquished jurisdiction under Article 30 or when the case has been referred to it under Article 43;
b. decide on issues referred to the Court by the Committee of Ministers in accordance with Article 46, paragraph 4; and
c. consider requests for advisory opinions submitted under Article 47.

Article 32 – Jurisdiction of the Court

1. The jurisdiction of the Court shall extend to all matters concerning the interpretation and application of the Convention and the protocols thereto which are referred to it as provided in Articles 33, 34, 46 and 47.
2. In the event of dispute as to whether the Court has jurisdiction, the Court shall decide.

Article 33 – Inter-State cases

Any High Contracting Party may refer to the Court any alleged breach of the provisions of the Convention and the protocols thereto by another High Contracting Party.

Article 34 – Individual applications

Chart of Declarations under former Articles 25 and 46 of the ECHR

The Court may receive applications from any person, non-governmental organisation or group of individuals claiming to be the victim of a violation by one of the High Contracting Parties of the rights set forth in the Convention or the protocols thereto. The High Contracting Parties undertake not to hinder in any way the effective exercise of this right.

Article 35 – Admissibility criteria

1. The Court may only deal with the matter after all domestic remedies have been exhausted, according to the generally recognised rules of international law, and within a period of six months from the date on which the final decision was taken.
2. The Court shall not deal with any application submitted under Article 34 that
   a. is anonymous; or
   b. is substantially the same as a matter that has already been examined by the Court or has already been submitted to another procedure of international investigation or settlement and contains no relevant new information.
3. The Court shall declare inadmissible any individual application submitted under Article 34 if it considers that :
   a. the application is incompatible with the provisions of the Convention or the Protocols thereto, manifestly ill-founded, or an abuse of the right of individual application; or
   b. the applicant has not suffered a significant disadvantage, unless respect for human rights as defined in the Convention and the Protocols thereto requires an examination of the application on the merits and provided that no case may be rejected on this ground which has not been duly considered by a domestic tribunal.
4. The Court shall reject any application which it considers inadmissible under this Article. It may do so at any stage of the proceedings.

Article 36 – Third party intervention

1. In all cases before a Chamber or the Grand Chamber, a High Contracting Party one of whose nationals is an applicant shall have the right to submit written comments and to take part in hearings.
2. The President of the Court may, in the interest of the proper administration of justice, invite any High Contracting Party which is not a party to the proceedings or any person concerned who is not the applicant to submit written comments or take part in hearings.
3. In all cases before a Chamber or the Grand Chamber, the Council of Europe Commissioner for Human Rights may submit written comments and take part in hearings.

Article 37 – Striking out applications

1. The Court may at any stage of the proceedings decide to strike an application out of its list of cases where the circumstances lead to the conclusion that:

a. the applicant does not intend to pursue his application; or
b. the matter has been resolved; or
c. for any other reason established by the Court, it is no longer justified to continue the examination of the application.

2. However, the Court shall continue the examination of the application if respect for human rights as defined in the Convention and the protocols thereto so requires.

3. The Court may decide to restore an application to its list of cases if it considers that the circumstances justify such a course.

Article 38 – Examination of the case

The Court shall examine the case together with the representatives of the parties and, if need be, undertake an investigation, for the effective conduct of which the High Contracting Parties concerned shall furnish all necessary facilities.

Article 39 – Friendly settlements

1. At any stage of the proceedings, the Court may place itself at the disposal of the parties concerned with a view to securing a friendly settlement of the matter on the basis of respect for human rights as defined in the Convention and the Protocols thereto.
2. Proceedings conducted under paragraph 1 shall be confidential.
3. If a friendly settlement is effected, the Court shall strike the case out of its list by means of a decision which shall be confined to a brief statement of the facts and of the solution reached.
4. This decision shall be transmitted to the Committee of Ministers, which shall supervise the execution of the terms of the friendly settlement as set out in the decision.

Article 40 – Public hearings and access to documents

1. Hearings shall be in public unless the Court in exceptional circumstances decides otherwise.
2. Documents deposited with the Registrar shall be accessible to the public unless the President of the Court decides otherwise.

Article 41 – Just satisfaction

If the Court finds that there has been a violation of the Convention or the protocols thereto, and if the internal law of the High Contracting Party concerned allows only partial reparation to be made, the Court shall, if necessary, afford just satisfaction to the injured party.

Article 42 – Judgments of Chambers

Judgments of Chambers shall become final in accordance with the provisions of Article 44, paragraph 2.

Article 43 – Referral to the Grand Chamber

1. Within a period of three months from the date of the judgment of the Chamber, any party to the case may, in exceptional cases, request that the case be referred to the Grand Chamber.
2. A panel of five judges of the Grand Chamber shall accept the request if the case raises a serious question affecting the interpretation or application of the Convention or the protocols thereto, or a serious issue of general importance.
3. If the panel accepts the request, the Grand Chamber shall decide the case by means of a judgment.

Article 44 – Final judgments

1. The judgment of the Grand Chamber shall be final.
2. The judgment of a Chamber shall become final:
   a. when the parties declare that they will not request that the case be referred to the Grand Chamber; or
   b. three months after the date of the judgment, if reference of the case to the Grand Chamber has not been requested; or
   c. when the panel of the Grand Chamber rejects the request to refer under Article 43.
3. The final judgment shall be published.

Article 45 – Reasons for judgments and decisions

1. Reasons shall be given for judgments as well as for decisions declaring applications admissible or inadmissible.
2. If a judgment does not represent, in whole or in part, the unanimous opinion of the judges, any judge shall be entitled to deliver a separate opinion.

Article 46 – Binding force and execution of judgments

1. The High Contracting Parties undertake to abide by the final judgment of the Court in any case to which they are parties.

2. The final judgment of the Court shall be transmitted to the Committee of Ministers, which shall supervise its execution.
3. If the Committee of Ministers considers that the supervision of the execution of a final judgment is hindered by a problem of interpretation of the judgment, it may refer the matter to the Court for a ruling on the question of interpretation. A referral decision shall require a majority vote of two thirds of the representatives entitled to sit on the Committee.
4. If the Committee of Ministers considers that a High Contracting Party refuses to abide by a final judgment in a case to which it is a party, it may, after serving formal notice on that Party and by decision adopted by a majority vote of two thirds of the representatives entitled to sit on the Committee, refer to the Court the question whether that Party has failed to fulfil its obligation under paragraph 1.
5. If the Court finds a violation of paragraph 1, it shall refer the case to the Committee of Ministers for consideration of the measures to be taken. If the Court finds no violation of paragraph 1, it shall refer the case to the Committee of Ministers, which shall close its examination of the case.

Article 47 – Advisory opinions

1. The Court may, at the request of the Committee of Ministers, give advisory opinions on legal questions concerning the interpretation of the Convention and the protocols thereto.
2. Such opinions shall not deal with any question relating to the content or scope of the rights or freedoms defined in Section I of the Convention and the protocols thereto, or with any other question which the Court or the Committee of Ministers might have to consider in consequence of any such proceedings as could be instituted in accordance with the Convention.
3. Decisions of the Committee of Ministers to request an advisory opinion of the Court shall require a majority vote of the representatives entitled to sit on the Committee.

Article 48 – Advisory jurisdiction of the Court

The Court shall decide whether a request for an advisory opinion submitted by the Committee of Ministers is within its competence as defined in Article 47.

Article 49 – Reasons for advisory opinions

1. Reasons shall be given for advisory opinions of the Court.

2. If the advisory opinion does not represent, in whole or in part, the unanimous opinion of the judges, any judge shall be entitled to deliver a separate opinion.
3. Advisory opinions of the Court shall be communicated to the Committee of Ministers.

Article 50 – Expenditure on the Court

The expenditure on the Court shall be borne by the Council of Europe.

Article 51 – Privileges and immunities of judges

The judges shall be entitled, during the exercise of their functions, to the privileges and immunities provided for in Article 40 of the Statute of the Council of Europe and in the agreements made thereunder.

Section III – Miscellaneous provisions

Article 52 – Inquiries by the Secretary General

On receipt of a request from the Secretary General of the Council of Europe any High Contracting Party shall furnish an explanation of the manner in which its internal law ensures the effective implementation of any of the provisions of the Convention.

Article 53 – Safeguard for existing human rights

Nothing in this Convention shall be construed as limiting or derogating from any of the human rights and fundamental freedoms which may be ensured under the laws of any High Contracting Party or under any other agreement to which it is a Party.

Article 54 – Powers of the Committee of Ministers

Nothing in this Convention shall prejudice the powers conferred on the Committee of Ministers by the Statute of the Council of Europe.

Article 55 – Exclusion of other means of dispute settlement

The High Contracting Parties agree that, except by special agreement, they will not avail themselves of treaties, conventions or declarations in force between them for the purpose of submitting, by way of petition, a dispute arising out of the interpretation or application of this Convention to a means of settlement other than those provided for in this Convention.

Article 56 – Territorial application

1. Any State may at the time of its ratification or at any time thereafter declare by notification addressed to the Secretary General of the Council of Europe that the present Convention shall, subject to paragraph 4 of this Article, extend to all or any of the territories for whose international relations it is responsible.
2. The Convention shall extend to the territory or territories named in the notification as from the thirtieth day after the receipt of this notification by the Secretary General of the Council of Europe.
3. The provisions of this Convention shall be applied in such territories with due regard, however, to local requirements.
4. Any State which has made a declaration in accordance with paragraph 1 of this article may at any time thereafter declare on behalf of one or more of the territories to which the declaration relates that it accepts the competence of the Court to receive applications from individuals, non-governmental organisations or groups of individuals as provided by Article 34 of the Convention.

Article 57 – Reservations

1. Any State may, when signing this Convention or when depositing its instrument of ratification, make a reservation in respect of any particular provision of the Convention to the extent that any law then in force in its territory is not in conformity with the provision. Reservations of a general character shall not be permitted under this article.
2. Any reservation made under this article shall contain a brief statement of the law concerned.

Article 58 – Denunciation

1. A High Contracting Party may denounce the present Convention only after the expiry of five years from the date on which it became a party to it and after six months' notice contained in a notification addressed to the Secretary General of the Council of Europe, who shall inform the other High Contracting Parties.
2. Such a denunciation shall not have the effect of releasing the High Contracting Party concerned from its obligations under this Convention in respect of any act which, being capable of constituting a violation of such obligations, may have been performed by it before the date at which the denunciation became effective.
3. Any High Contracting Party which shall cease to be a member of the Council of Europe shall cease to be a Party to this Convention under the same conditions.

4. The Convention may be denounced in accordance with the provisions of the preceding paragraphs in respect of any territory to which it has been declared to extend under the terms of Article 56.

Article 59 – Signature and ratification

1. This Convention shall be open to the signature of the members of the Council of Europe. It shall be ratified. Ratifications shall be deposited with the Secretary General of the Council of Europe.
2. The European Union may accede to this Convention.
3. The present Convention shall come into force after the deposit of ten instruments of ratification.
4. As regards any signatory ratifying subsequently, the Convention shall come into force at the date of the deposit of its instrument of ratification.
5. The Secretary General of the Council of Europe shall notify all the members of the Council of Europe of the entry into force of the Convention, the names of the High Contracting Parties who have ratified it, and the deposit of all instruments of ratification which may be effected subsequently.

Done at Rome this 4th day of November 1950, in English and French, both texts being equally authentic, in a single copy which shall remain deposited in the archives of the Council of Europe. The Secretary General shall transmit certified copies to each of the signatories.

E. Protocol No. 11

Article 1 – Protection of property

Every natural or legal person is entitled to the peaceful enjoyment of his possessions. No one shall be deprived of his possessions except in the public interest and subject to the conditions provided for by law and by the general principles of international law.
The preceding provisions shall not, however, in any way impair the right of a State to enforce such laws as it deems necessary to control the use of property in accordance with the general interest or to secure the payment of taxes or other contributions or penalties.

Article 2 – Right to education

No person shall be denied the right to education. In the exercise of any functions which it assumes in relation to education and to teaching, the State shall respect the right of parents to ensure such education and teaching in conformity with their own religious and philosophical convictions.

Article 3 – Right to free elections

The High Contracting Parties undertake to hold free elections at reasonable intervals by secret ballot, under conditions which will ensure the free expression of the opinion of the people in the choice of the legislature.

Article 4 – Territorial application

Any High Contracting Party may at the time of signature or ratification or at any time thereafter communicate to the Secretary General of the Council of Europe a declaration stating the extent to which it undertakes that the provisions of the present Protocol shall apply to such of the territories for the international relations of which it is responsible as are named therein.
Any High Contracting Party which has communicated a declaration in virtue of the preceding paragraph may from time to time communicate a further declaration modifying the terms of any former declaration or terminating the application of the provisions of this Protocol in respect of any territory.
A declaration made in accordance with this article shall be deemed to have been made in accordance with paragraph 1 of Article 56 of the Convention.

Article 5 – Relationship to the Convention

As between the High Contracting Parties the provisions of Articles 1, 2, 3 and 4 of this Protocol shall be regarded as additional articles to the Convention and all the provisions of the Convention shall apply accordingly.

Article 6 – Signature and ratification

This Protocol shall be open for signature by the members of the Council of Europe, who are the signatories of the Convention; it shall be ratified at the same time as or after the ratification of the Convention. It shall enter into force after the deposit of ten instruments of ratification. As regards any signatory ratifying subsequently, the Protocol shall enter into force at the date of the deposit of its instrument of ratification.

The instruments of ratification shall be deposited with the Secretary General of the Council of Europe, who will notify all members of the names of those who have ratified.
Done at Paris on the 20th day of March 1952, in English and French, both texts being equally authentic, in a single copy which shall remain deposited in the archives of the Council of Europe. The Secretary General shall transmit certified copies to each of the signatory governments.

F. Protocol No. 14

Article 1

Paragraph 2 of Article 22 of the Convention shall be deleted.

Article 2

Article 23 of the Convention shall be amended to read as follows:
"Article 23 – Terms of office and dismissal
1. The judges shall be elected for a period of nine years. They may not be re-elected.
2. The terms of office of judges shall expire when they reach the age of 70.
3. The judges shall hold office until replaced. They shall, however, continue to deal with such cases as they already have under consideration.
4. No judge may be dismissed from office unless the other judges decide by a majority of two-thirds that that judge has ceased to fulfil the required conditions."

Article 3

Article 24 of the Convention shall be deleted.

Article 4

Article 25 of the Convention shall become Article 24 and its text shall be amended to read as follows:
"Article 24 – Registry and rapporteurs
1. The Court shall have a registry, the functions and organisation of which shall be laid down in the rules of the Court.
2. When sitting in a single-judge formation, the Court shall be assisted by rapporteurs who shall function under the authority of the President of the Court. They shall form part of the Court's registry."

Article 5

Article 26 of the Convention shall become Article 25 ("Plenary Court") and its text shall be amended as follows:

1. At the end of paragraph d, the comma shall be replaced by a semi-colon and the word "and" shall be deleted.

2. At the end of paragraph e, the full stop shall be replaced by a semi-colon.

3. A new paragraph f shall be added which shall read as follows:

"f. make any request under Article 26, paragraph 2."

Article 6

Article 27 of the Convention shall become Article 26 and its text shall be amended to read as follows:

"Article 26 – Single-judge formation, committees, Chambers and Grand Chamber

1. To consider cases brought before it, the Court shall sit in a single-judge formation, in committees of three judges, in Chambers of seven judges and in a Grand Chamber of seventeen judges. The Court's Chambers shall set up committees for a fixed period of time.

2. At the request of the plenary Court, the Committee of Ministers may, by a unanimous decision and for a fixed period, reduce to five the number of judges of the Chambers.

3. When sitting as a single judge, a judge shall not examine any application against the High Contracting Party in respect of which that judge has been elected.

4. There shall sit as an ex officio member of the Chamber and the Grand Chamber the judge elected in respect of the High Contracting Party concerned. If there is none or if that judge is unable to sit, a person chosen by the President of the Court from a list submitted in advance by that Party shall sit in the capacity of judge.

5. The Grand Chamber shall also include the President of the Court, the Vice-Presidents, the Presidents of the Chambers and other judges chosen in accordance with the rules of the Court. When a case is referred to the Grand Chamber under Article 43, no judge from the Chamber which rendered the judgment shall sit in the Grand Chamber, with the exception of the President of the Chamber and the judge who sat in respect of the High Contracting Party concerned."

Article 7

After the new Article 26, a new Article 27 shall be inserted into the Convention, which shall read as follows:

"Article 27 – Competence of single judges

1. A single judge may declare inadmissible or strike out of the Court's list of cases an application submitted under Article 34, where such a decision can be taken without further examination.
2. The decision shall be final.
3. If the single judge does not declare an application inadmissible or strike it out, that judge shall forward it to a committee or to a Chamber for further examination."

Article 8

Article 28 of the Convention shall be amended to read as follows:
"Article 28 – Competence of committees
1. In respect of an application submitted under Article 34, a committee may, by a unanimous vote,
a. declare it inadmissible or strike it out of its list of cases, where such decision can be taken without further examination; or
b. declare it admissible and render at the same time a judgment on the merits, if the underlying question in the case, concerning the interpretation or the application of the Convention or the Protocols thereto, is already the subject of well-established case-law of the Court.
2. Decisions and judgments under paragraph 1 shall be final.
3. If the judge elected in respect of the High Contracting Party concerned is not a member of the committee, the committee may at any stage of the proceedings invite that judge to take the place of one of the members of the committee, having regard to all relevant factors, including whether that Party has contested the application of the procedure under paragraph 1.b."

Article 9

Article 29 of the Convention shall be amended as follows:
1. Paragraph 1 shall be amended to read as follows: "If no decision is taken under Article 27 or 28, or no judgment rendered under Article 28, a Chamber shall decide on the admissibility and merits of individual applications submitted under Article 34. The decision on admissibility may be taken separately."
2. At the end of paragraph 2 a new sentence shall be added which shall read as follows: "The decision on admissibility shall be taken separately unless the Court, in exceptional cases, decides otherwise."
3. Paragraph 3 shall be deleted.

Article 10

Article 31 of the Convention shall be amended as follows:

1. At the end of paragraph a, the word “and” shall be deleted.

2. Paragraph b shall become paragraph c and a new paragraph b shall be inserted and shall read as follows:

“b. decide on issues referred to the Court by the Committee of Ministers in accordance with Article 46, paragraph 4; and”.

Article 11

Article 32 of the Convention shall be amended as follows:

At the end of paragraph 1, a comma and the number 46 shall be inserted after the number 34.

Article 12

Paragraph 3 of Article 35 of the Convention shall be amended to read as follows:

“3. The Court shall declare inadmissible any individual application submitted under Article 34 if it considers that :

a. the application is incompatible with the provisions of the Convention or the Protocols thereto, manifestly ill-founded, or an abuse of the right of individual application; or

b. the applicant has not suffered a significant disadvantage, unless respect for human rights as defined in the Convention and the Protocols thereto requires an examination of the application on the merits and provided that no case may be rejected on this ground which has not been duly considered by a domestic tribunal.”

Article 13

A new paragraph 3 shall be added at the end of Article 36 of the Convention, which shall read as follows:

“3. In all cases before a Chamber or the Grand Chamber, the Council of Europe Commissioner for Human Rights may submit written comments and take part in hearings.”

Article 14

Article 38 of the Convention shall be amended to read as follows:

“Article 38 – Examination of the case

The Court shall examine the case together with the representatives of the parties and, if need be, undertake an investigation, for the effective conduct of which the High Contracting Parties concerned shall furnish all necessary facilities.”

Article 15

Article 39 of the Convention shall be amended to read as follows:

"Article 39 – Friendly settlements

1. At any stage of the proceedings, the Court may place itself at the disposal of the parties concerned with a view to securing a friendly settlement of the matter on the basis of respect for human rights as defined in the Convention and the Protocols thereto.

2. Proceedings conducted under paragraph 1 shall be confidential.

3. If a friendly settlement is effected, the Court shall strike the case out of its list by means of a decision which shall be confined to a brief statement of the facts and of the solution reached.

4. This decision shall be transmitted to the Committee of Ministers, which shall supervise the execution of the terms of the friendly settlement as set out in the decision."

Article 16

Article 46 of the Convention shall be amended to read as follows:

"Article 46 – Binding force and execution of judgments

1. The High Contracting Parties undertake to abide by the final judgment of the Court in any case to which they are parties.

2. The final judgment of the Court shall be transmitted to the Committee of Ministers, which shall supervise its execution.

3. If the Committee of Ministers considers that the supervision of the execution of a final judgment is hindered by a problem of interpretation of the judgment, it may refer the matter to the Court for a ruling on the question of interpretation. A referral decision shall require a majority vote of two thirds of the representatives entitled to sit on the Committee.

4. If the Committee of Ministers considers that a High Contracting Party refuses to abide by a final judgment in a case to which it is a party, it may, after serving formal notice on that Party and by decision adopted by a majority vote of two thirds of the representatives entitled to sit on the Committee, refer to the Court the question whether that Party has failed to fulfil its obligation under paragraph 1.

5. If the Court finds a violation of paragraph 1, it shall refer the case to the Committee of Ministers for consideration of the measures to be taken. If the Court finds no violation of paragraph 1, it shall refer the case to the Committee of Ministers, which shall close its examination of the case."

Article 17

Article 59 of the Convention shall be amended as follows:

1. A new paragraph 2 shall be inserted which shall read as follows:
“2. The European Union may accede to this Convention.”
2. Paragraphs 2, 3 and 4 shall become paragraphs 3, 4 and 5 respectively.
Final and transitional provisions

Article 18

1. This Protocol shall be open for signature by member States of the Council of Europe signatories to the Convention, which may express their consent to be bound by
a. signature without reservation as to ratification, acceptance or approval; or
b. signature subject to ratification, acceptance or approval, followed by ratification, acceptance or approval.
2. The instruments of ratification, acceptance or approval shall be deposited with the Secretary General of the Council of Europe.

Article 19

This Protocol shall enter into force on the first day of the month following the expiration of a period of three months after the date on which all Parties to the Convention have expressed their consent to be bound by the Protocol, in accordance with the provisions of Article 18.

Article 20

1. From the date of the entry into force of this Protocol, its provisions shall apply to all applications pending before the Court as well as to all judgments whose execution is under supervision by the Committee of Ministers.
2. The new admissibility criterion inserted by Article 12 of this Protocol in Article 35, paragraph 3.b of the Convention, shall not apply to applications declared admissible before the entry into force of the Protocol. In the two years following the entry into force of this Protocol, the new admissibility criterion may only be applied by Chambers and the Grand Chamber of the Court.

Article 21

The term of office of judges serving their first term of office on the date of entry into force of this Protocol shall be extended ipso jure so as to amount to a total period of nine years. The other judges shall complete their term of office, which shall be extended ipso jure by two years.

G. Protocol No. 15

Article 1

At the end of the preamble to the Convention, a new recital shall be added, which shall read as follows:
“Affirming that the High Contracting Parties, in accordance with the principle of subsidiarity, have the primary responsibility to secure the rights and freedoms defined in this Convention and the Protocols thereto, and that in doing so they enjoy a margin of appreciation, subject to the supervisory jurisdiction of the European Court of Human Rights established by this Convention,”.

Article 2

1 In Article 21 of the Convention, a new paragraph 2 shall be inserted, which shall read as follows: “Candidates shall be less than 65 years of age at the date by which the list of three candidates has been requested by the Parliamentary Assembly, further to Article 22.”
2 Paragraphs 2 and 3 of Article 21 of the Convention shall become paragraphs 3 and 4 of Article 21 respectively.
3 Paragraph 2 of Article 23 of the Convention shall be deleted. Paragraphs 3 and 4 of Article 23 shall become paragraphs 2 and 3 of Article 23 respectively.

Article 3

In Article 30 of the Convention, the words “unless one of the parties to the case objects” shall be deleted.

Article 4

In Article 35, paragraph 1 of the Convention, the words “within a period of six months” shall be replaced by the words “within a period of four months”.

Article 5

In Article 35, paragraph 3, sub-paragraph b of the Convention, the words “and provided that no case may be rejected on this ground which has not been duly considered by a domestic tribunal” shall be deleted.

Final and transitional provisions

Article 6

1 This Protocol shall be open for signature by the High Contracting Parties to the Convention, which may express their consent to be bound by:

a signature without reservation as to ratification, acceptance or approval; or

b signature subject to ratification, acceptance or approval, followed by ratification, acceptance or approval.

2 The instruments of ratification, acceptance or approval shall be deposited with the Secretary General of the Council of Europe.

Article 7

This Protocol shall enter into force on the first day of the month following the expiration of a period of three months after the date on which all High Contracting Parties to the Convention have expressed their consent to be bound by the Protocol, in accordance with the provisions of Article 6.

Article 8

1 The amendments introduced by Article 2 of this Protocol shall apply only to candidates on lists submitted to the Parliamentary Assembly by the High Contracting Parties under Article 22 of the Convention after the entry into force of this Protocol.

2 The amendment introduced by Article 3 of this Protocol shall not apply to any pending case in which one of the parties has objected, prior to the date of entry into force of this Protocol, to a proposal by a Chamber of the Court to relinquish jurisdiction in favour of the Grand Chamber.

3 Article 4 of this Protocol shall enter into force following the expiration of a period of six months after the date of entry into force of this Protocol. Article 4 of this Protocol shall not apply to applications in respect of which the final decision within the meaning of Article 35, paragraph 1 of the Convention was taken prior to the date of entry into force of Article 4 of this Protocol.

4 All other provisions of this Protocol shall apply from its date of entry into force, in accordance with the provisions of Article 7.

Article 9

The Secretary General of the Council of Europe shall notify the Member States of the Council of Europe and the other High Contracting Parties to the Convention of:

a any signature;

b the deposit of any instrument of ratification, acceptance or approval;

c the date of entry into force of this Protocol in accordance with Article 7; and

d any other act, notification or communication relating to this Protocol.

In witness whereof, the undersigned, being duly authorised thereto, have signed this Protocol.

Done at Strasbourg, this 24th day of June 2013, in English and in French, both texts being equally authentic, in a single copy which shall be deposited in the archives of the Council of Europe. The Secretary General of the Council of Europe shall transmit certified copies to each member State of the Council of Europe and to the other High Contracting Parties to the Convention.

H. Protocol No. 16

Article 1

1. Highest courts and tribunals of a High Contracting Party, as specified in accordance with Article 10, may request the Court to give advisory opinions on questions of principle relating to the interpretation or application of the rights and freedoms defined in the Convention or the protocols thereto.
2. The requesting court or tribunal may seek an advisory opinion only in the context of a case pending before it.
3. The requesting court or tribunal shall give reasons for its request and shall provide the relevant legal and factual background of the pending case.

Article 2

1. A panel of five judges of the Grand Chamber shall decide whether to accept the request for an advisory opinion, having regard to Article 1. The panel shall give reasons for any refusal to accept the request.
2. If the panel accepts the request, the Grand Chamber shall deliver the advisory opinion.
3. The panel and the Grand Chamber, as referred to in the preceding paragraphs, shall include ex officio the judge elected in respect of the High Contracting Party to which the requesting court or tribunal pertains. If there is none or if that judge is unable to sit, a person chosen by the President of the Court from a list submitted in advance by that Party shall sit in the capacity of judge.

Article 3

The Council of Europe Commissioner for Human Rights and the High Contracting Party to which the requesting court or tribunal pertains shall have the right to submit written comments and take part in any hearing. The President of the Court may, in the interest of the proper administration of justice, invite any other High Contracting Party or person also to submit written comments or take part in any hearing.

Article 4

1. Reasons shall be given for advisory opinions.
2. If the advisory opinion does not represent, in whole or in part, the unanimous opinion of the judges, any judge shall be entitled to deliver a separate opinion.
3. Advisory opinions shall be communicated to the requesting court or tribunal and to the High Contracting Party to which that court or tribunal pertains.
4. Advisory opinions shall be published.

Article 5

Advisory opinions shall not be binding.

Article 6

As between the High Contracting Parties the provisions of Articles 1 to 5 of this Protocol shall be regarded as additional articles to the Convention, and all the provisions of the Convention shall apply accordingly.

Article 7

1. This Protocol shall be open for signature by the High Contracting Parties to the Convention, which may express their consent to be bound by:

a. signature without reservation as to ratification, acceptance or approval; or

b. signature subject to ratification, acceptance or approval, followed by ratification, acceptance or approval.

2. The instruments of ratification, acceptance or approval shall be deposited with the Secretary General of the Council of Europe.

Article 8

1. This Protocol shall enter into force on the first day of the month following the expiration of a period of three months after the date on which ten High Contracting Parties to the Convention have expressed their consent to be bound by the Protocol in accordance with the provisions of Article 7
2. In respect of any High Contracting Party to the Convention which subsequently expresses its

consent to be bound by it, the Protocol shall enter into force on the first day of the month following the expiration of a period of three months after the date of the expression of its consent to be bound by the Protocol in accordance with the provisions of Article 7.

Article 9

No reservation may be made under Article 57 of the Convention in respect of the provisions of this Protocol.

Article 10

Each High Contracting Party to the Convention shall, at the time of signature or when depositing its instrument of ratification, acceptance or approval, by means of a declaration addressed to the Secretary General of the Council of Europe, indicate the courts or tribunals that it designates for the purposes of Article 1, paragraph 1, of this Protocol. This declaration may be modified at any later date and in the same manner.

Article 11

The Secretary General of the Council of Europe shall notify the member States of the Council of Europe and the other High Contracting Parties to the Convention of:

a. any signature;

b. the deposit of any instrument of ratification, acceptance or approval;

c. any date of entry into force of this Protocol in accordance with Article 8;

d. any declaration made in accordance with Article 10; and

e. any other act, notification or communication relating to this Protocol.

Bibliography

Bertrand M., Warner D., A New Charter for Worldwide Organization? (1995)

Collected Edition of the 'Travaux Préparatoires' of the European Convention on Human Rights Vol. I: Preparatory Commission of the Council of Europe, Committee of Ministers, Consultative Assembly, II May-8 September 1949

Collected Edition of the "Travaux Préparatoires" of the European Convention on Human Rights, Volume IV, The Hague, (1977)

Cook R.J., Human Rights of Women - National and International Perspectives (1994)

Council of Europe, Collected Texts (1994)

De Salvia M.,Villinger M. E., The birth of European Human Rights Law (1998)

Di Frederico G., The EU Charter of Fundamental RIghts: From Declaration to Binding Instrument (2009)

Emmerson B., Ashworth A.,Macdonald A., Human Rights and Criminal Justice (2012)

Ganten T.O., Die Drittwirkung der Grundfreiheiten (2000)

Gomien D., Short guide to the European Convention on Human Rights (2005)

Greer S., The European Convention on human Rights: Achievements and Prospects (2006)

Grabenwarter C./Pabel K., Europäische Menschenrechtskonvention: Ein Studienbuch (2012)

Foster Nigel, EU Law - Directions (2010)

Freeman M.A., Rudolf B., Chinkin C., The UN Convention On The Elimination of All Forms of Discrimination Against Women (2012)

Frenz W., Handbuch Europarecht, Band 5: Wirkungen und Rechtsschutz (2010)

Jacobs F.G., White R., Ovey C., The European Convention on Human Rights (2010)

Janis M., Kay R., Bradley A., European Human Rights Law (2008)

Jayawickrama N., The Judicial Application of Human Rights Law (2002)

Johnson M. G./Symonides J., The Universal Declaration of Human Rights: A history of its creations and implementation 1948 - 1998 (1998)

Jordan R.S., International Organizations: A Comparative Approach to the Management of Cooperation (2001)

Kesselman et al., European Politics in Transition (2005)

Kleinsorge Tanja E.J., Council of Europe (2010)

Kicker R., The Council of Europe: Pioneer and Guarantor for Human Rights and Democracy (2010)

Leach P., Taking a Case to the European Court of Human Rights (2011)

Legg A., The Margin of Appreciation in International Human Rights Law, Deference and Proportionality (2012)

Letsas G., A theory of Interpretation of the European Convention on Human Rights (2007)

Lipgens W., Loth W., Documents on the History of European Integration, Volume 3 'The struggle for European Union by political Parties and Pressure Groups in Western Countries 1945 - 1950
Loveland I., Constitutional Law, Administrative Law and Human Rights: A critical introduction (2012)
Macdonald R.St.J., Matscher F., Petzold H., The European System for the Protection of Human Rights. (1993)
Nijhoff M., Council of Europe: Collected Edition of the "travaux Préparatoires" of the European Convention on Human Rights Volume VI (1985)
Peterson M. J., The United Nations General Assembly (2006)
Robertson A., Council of Europe - Collected edition of the "travaux préparatoires" of the ECHR, (The Hague: Nijhoff M. (1975)
Roca J.G., Santolaya P., Europe of Rights: A compendium on the European Convention of Human Rights (2008)
Smith R.K.M., Van den Anker C., The essentials of human rights (2005)
Slomanson W.R., Fundamental Perspectives on International Law (2011)
The United Nations Department of Public Information, The United Nations and Human Rights 1945 - 1995, Volume VII (1995)
The United Nations, Basic facts about the United Nations (2004)
Van Dijk P./Van Hoof G.J.H., Theory and Practice of the European Convention on Human Rights (1998)

Journals and Reports

Gray C., European Convention on Human Rights - Freedom of Expression and the Thalidomide Case, The Cambridge Law Journal, Volume 38 (1979)
Helfer L.R., Redesigning the European Court of Human Rights: Embeddedness as a Deep Structural Principle of the European Human Rights Regime, Vol. 19/1, 125-129, The European Journal of International Law (2008)
Hilson C., Global Constitutionalism - The margin of appreciation, domestic irregularity and domestic court rulings in ECHR environmental jurisprudence: Global legal pluralism in action, Cambridge Law Journal, Volume 2 (2013)
Madhavi S., Piercing the Veil, Yale Law Journal, Volume 112 (2003)
Sakyrakis S., Proportionality: An Assault on Human Rights?,Jean Monnet Working Paper 09/08 (2012)
Spencer J.R., Extradition, the European Arrest Warrant and Human Rights, The Cambridge Law Journal, Volume 72 (2013)

Reports of Judgments of the International Court of Justice in the Case of Democratic Republic of the Congo v. Uganda, 19.12.2005

Internet resources

http://ap.ohchr.org/documents/alldocs.aspx?doc_id=5820
http://centers.law.nyu.edu/jeanmonnet/papers/08/080901.pdf
http://www.coe.int/t/dghl/cooperation/lisbonnetwork/themis/echr/paper2_en.asp
http://echr.coe.int/Documents/Courts_advisory_jurisdiction_ENG.pdf
http://www.echr.coe.int/Documents/Stats_analysis_2012_ENG.pdf
http://echr.coe.int/NR/rdonlyres/C3804E16-817B-46D5-A51F-0AC1A8E0FB8D/0/DG2ENHRHAND022004.pdf
http://www.echr.coe.int/Pages/home.aspx?p=basictexts&c=#n13739063294958599503665_pointer
http://www.conventions.coe.int/Treaty/Commun/ChercheSig.asp NT=213&CM=8&DF=15/12/2013&CL=ENG
http://www.conventions.coe.int/Treaty/Commun ChercheSig.aspNT=214&CM=8&DF=15/12/2013&CL=ENG
http://www.equalityhumanrights.com/legal-and-policy/legal-updates/the-smith-case/
http://fds.oup.com/www.oup.com/pdf/13/9780199203437.pdf
http://hub.coe.int/web/coe-portal/european-union?dynLink=true&fromArticleId=&dlgroupId=10226&layoutId=772
http://www.journal-iostudies.org/sites/journal-iostudies.org/files/JIOSfinal_3_1.pdf
http://library.law.yale.edu/collected-travaux-preparatoires
http://www.ohchr.org/EN/HRBodies/HRC/ComplaintProcedure/Pages/HRCComplaintProcedureIndex.aspx
http://www.theguardian.com/world/2013/jul/30/abortion-ireland-becomes-legal-circumstances
http://www.theguardian.com/law/2012/apr/19/european-court-of-human-rights-human-rights
http://www.un.org/en/documents/charter/
http://www.un.org/en/events/humanrightsday/2011/sg.shtml
http://www.unric.org/en/uk-a-ireland-news-archive/28258-key-statistics-on-violence-against-women-and-girls-
http://www.who.int/mediacentre/factsheets/fs239/en/

Table of cases

European Court of Human Rights

A,B,C v. Ireland, judgment of 16.12.2010

Airey v. Ireland, judgment of 09.10.1979

Al-Skeini and others v. The United Kingdom, judgment of 07.07.2011

Aktivar and others v. Turkey, judgment of 16.09.1996

Bankovic and others v. Belgium, the Czech Republic, Denmark, France, Germany, Greece, Hungary, Iceland, Italy, Luxembourg, the Netherlands, Norway, Poland, Portugal, Spain, Turkey and the United Kingdom, judgment of 12.12.2001

Buckley v. the United Kingdom, judgment of 25.09.1996

Chassagnou and Others v. France, judgment of 29.04.1999

Christine Goodwin v. the United Kingdom, judgment of 11.07.2002

Cossey v. the United Kingdom, judgment of 27.09.1990

Cypress v. Turkey, judgment of 10.05.2001

Dudgeon v. the United Kingdom, judgment of 22.10.1981

Earl and Countess Spencer v. United Kingdom, judgment of 16.01.1998

Engel and others v. the Netherlands, judgment of 08.06.1976

Eremia v. the Republic of Moldova, judgment of 28.05.2013

Evans v. the United KIngdom, judgment of 10.04.2007

Handyside v. The United Kingdom, judgment of 07.12.1976

Hatton and others v. the United Kingdom, judgment of 08.07.2003

Hirst v. the United Kingdom, judgment of 06.10.2005

I.G. v. Moldova, judgment of 15.05.2012

Ireland v. the United Kingdom, judgment of 18.01.1978

Loizidou v. Turkey, judgment of 18.12.1996

Malone v. the United Kingdom, judgment of 02.08.1984

Marckx v. Belgium, judgment of 13.06.1979

M.C. v. Bulgaria, judgment of 04.12.2003

Observer&Guardian v. the United Kingdom, judgment of 26.11.1991

Olsson v. Sweden, judgment of 24.03.1988

Prokopovich v. Russia, judgment of 18.11.2004

Rees v. The United Kingdom, judgment of 17.10.1986

RTBF v. Belgium, judgment of 29.3.2011

Sheffield and Horsham v. the United Kingdom, judgment of 30.07.1998

Soering v. the United Kingdom, judgment of 07.07.1989

Sunday Times v. the United Kingdom, judgment of 26.04.1979
Tyrer v. the United Kingdom, judgment of 25.04.1978
Tysiac v. Poland,judgment of 20.03.2007
Valieliené v. Lithuania, judgment of 26.03.2013
Vo v. France, judgment of 08.07.2004
X v. United Kingdom, judgment of 05.11.1981

European Court of Justice
Case 26-62, judgment of 05.02.1963
Case 11-70, judgment of 17.12.1970
Case 43-75, judgment of 08.04.1976

International Court of Justice
Case concerning United States diplomatic and consular staff in Tehran, judgment of 24.05.1980
Filartiga v. Pena-Irala, judgment of 06.06.1980
Nottebohm Case, judgment of 06.04.1955
South-West Africa Cases, judgment of 18.07.1966

Bundesverfassungsgericht Deutschland
BVerfGE 37, 271 (Solange I), 29.05.1974
BVerfGE 73, 339 (Solange II), 22.10.1986